1986

JAMES MACPHERSON

From the Portrait by Romney,
now at Belleville House, Kingussie, N.B.

THE LIFE AND LETTERS

OF

JAMES MACPHERSON

CONTAINING A PARTICULAR ACCOUNT OF HIS FAMOUS
QUARREL WITH Dr. JOHNSON, AND A SKETCH OF
THE ORIGIN AND INFLUENCE OF THE
OSSIANIC POEMS

BY

BAILEY SAUNDERS

GREENWOOD PRESS, PUBLISHERS
NEW YORK

Originally published in 1894
by Swan Sonnenschein & Co.

First Greenwood Reprinting 1969

SBN 8371-2390-9

PRINTED IN UNITED STATES OF AMERICA

PREFACE.

AMONG educated Englishmen Macpherson commonly passes for an audacious impostor who published his own compositions as the work of an ancient writer, and received due punishment at the hands of Dr. Johnson. The historians of literature compare him with Chatterton, and brand him as a forger. Even those who refrain from giving him a harsh name treat him with doubt and hesitation. An equal obscurity envelops his life and actions and the nature of his work; and the result of ignorance or misconception is that he has obtained something less than justice.

If none but the great deserved a biography, this book would not have been written. For Macpherson was in no sense a great man: he was a miscellaneous writer of considerable talent, a busy journalist, a member of parliament, an agent for an Indian prince, a popular and prosperous citizen; and, beyond the fact that he brought out the Ossianic poems at the age of twenty-five, he did little in the sixty years of his life that would entitle him to permanent remembrance. This work of his youth was, as he declared, translated from Gaelic fragments found in the Scottish Highlands. By its wonderful success, and its no less wonderful influence on literature, both in England and on the Continent, it gave him, in his own day, a world-wide reputation. Literary fashions have suffered many changes in the century that has passed since his death, and Macpherson's reputation no longer exists ; but his work retains an historical interest of a curious and unique character. It is strange evidence of the instability of literary fame that poems which, three generations ago, were everywhere in vogue and everywhere imitated—which appealed to the feelings of all the cultured classes in Europe, and excited the enthusiasm even of a Goethe, a Byron, and a Napoleon—should now be almost forgotten.

The origin, reception, and extraordinary effect

of the Ossianic poems form a chapter, hitherto
unwritten, in the literary history of the eighteenth century; and to attempt to write it is, I
trust, at least a respectable endeavour. I have
thrown it into the form of a biography because
the question of the authenticity of the poems
largely turns on Macpherson's actual proceedings, and his personal character and attainments; and thus it is that some interest still
attaches to the details of his life, so far as they
can be discovered.

While I believe that, on the whole, he has
been greatly slandered, he is certainly no hero;
and I hope that I am not afflicted, in regard
to him, with what has been called the *lues
boswelliana*, or the disease of admiration. I hope
also that I am free from any suspicion of
national prejudice; I have not the honour of
being a Scotsman. My curiosity about so wide
and perplexing a subject as the Ossianic controversy was aroused by an accident; and one
of the recognised ways of getting rid of a
burden is to write a book on it.

I have been fortunate in obtaining some information from unpublished sources in the British Museum and elsewhere. My best thanks are due to the Marquess of Abergavenny for kindly permitting me to make use of a series of Macpherson's letters preserved in the library at Eridge; and to Mr. Brewster Macpherson of Belleville for the reproduction of Romney's portrait of his ancestor. I am also grateful for assistance rendered by friends, notably by Miss Mary Grant (of Kilgraston) and by Mr. John Cameron Grant (of Glenmoriston).

May 21, 1894.

CONTENTS.

CONTENTS.

CHAPTER VI.

CHAPTER VII.

CHAPTER VIII.

CHAPTER IX.

CHAPTER X.

Chapter XI.

Chapter XII.

Chapter XIII.

Chapter XIV.

CHAPTER I.

The Ossianic Poems.—Their Character and Influence.—Macpherson.

In the middle of the eighteenth century a rumour went out from Edinburgh that the songs of an ancient poet, as great as Homer, had been discovered in the Highlands. Fragments of an heroic strain were, it was said, often to be heard in the valleys beyond the Grampians, or on the shores of the Hebrides; telling, in mournful verse, of the brave deeds of other days, of the battles of Fingal, a glorious king, and the woes of Ossian, his son, who was left, old and blind, to lament the friends of his youth. Those who were familiar with the barbarous speech of the country declared that these wild poems were of singular beauty, and sublime in their pathos; tradition assigned them to a dim antiquity; nay, if report were true, their forlorn author lived at the time when the Romans invaded the north, and his words had been handed down on the lips of the people for fifteen hundred years.

1

There are some who still believe in the
legend; nor is it unwelcome. Could we suppose
that the mountains, as we see them in an air of
soft mist and broken sunshine, are haunted by
the voices of an antique age, it would please our
fancy; even though a great magician has peopled
the moors and valleys with the creatures of
later romance. Who that has wandered in the
deserted glens, or by the rocky coast where the
tide swells among islets innumerable, would
not willingly dream that a tale of the times
of old lingers in the midst of that wild and
melancholy grandeur? that we hear its echo on
loch and hill, in the measured chant of the
boatmen, or in the song of the Highland lass
as she reaps in solitude—

> " Breaking the silence of the seas
> Among the farthest Hebrides.

> " Will no one tell me what she sings?
> Perhaps the plaintive numbers flow
> For old, unhappy, far-off things,
> And battles long ago."

If we feel that poetry is at home in the Highlands, it is a feeling inspired by the beauty of
nature; and the old fragments that were found
did, it seemed, truly reflect the best features of

a landscape now familiar.   But in the middle of
the eighteenth century there was little admiration for bleak mountains and rugged hills; and
at first the scenery of this wild poetry yielded to
its human interest, and its picture of ancient
life in a desolate country.   It was only in recent
years that the Highlands had been explored.
Their condition at the period of the rising in
'45, the independent rule of the chiefs, and
the rough life of the clans, are now matters
of general knowledge.   But for long after
the rising, and in spite of the efforts of the
English Government to establish communication with the south, the north of Scotland
was still, in the common report of the time,
a benighted region, wrapt in fog and storm.
Of the inhabitants little was known but that
they were men of great size and savage bearing, who in the service of their chiefs had
been trained from their youth to the pursuits
of war.   For the chiefs were reputed to be
sovereigns in the narrow valleys in which they
lived; they maintained in their fastnesses the
airs and manners of a rude court, and in all
things they were faithfully supported by their
followers, who formed standing armies, jealous

of their masters' rights, and always ready to defend them at the point of the sword. They and their fathers had always loved the clash of arms; and had not these hardy sons of the mountain but lately carried terror to the plains when they descended to fight for a lost cause? It was natural that their wild songs should breathe of the joys of battle, the glory of the victors, and the desolation of the conquered. Many gentle and noble traits in the character of the Highlanders were also reported; and these, too, it was said, were reflected in their poetry; as well as strange customs and superstitions elsewhere unknown. For they served their clans with a chivalrous devotion, and in life and death were faithful to old traditions.

To keep alive the martial spirit of their ancestors, the chiefs everywhere maintained bards and senachies, who at great festivals commemorated the deeds of the clan. Sometimes in the long nights of winter they would also recount the feats of ancient days; singing, as they supposed, the very words of the master himself, the prince of poets.

To this lonely Ossian, the last of his race, the bards looked back with a reverent affection;

and the songs and ballads which immemorial tradition assigned to him were treasured with peculiar care. The office of the bard, like that of his chief, was hereditary; the poetry which he had learned from his father, he taught in turn to his son; and thus he came to believe that Ossian was the fount and origin of all bardic inspiration; and that the best of the poems to be found in the Highlands had been composed by this great poet in an unknown antiquity.

As we see him in the old songs, sitting alone in his blindness, and filled with the remembrance of the friends whom he soon must follow, Ossian is certainly a figure that stirs the heart. "Happy are those," he murmurs, "who die in their youth, in the midst of their renown; they have not beheld the tombs of their friends, or failed to bend the bow of their strength." As for him, he is the voice of an age that is past. He recalls in his solitude the words of brother-bards in the days of song :—

"When bards are removed to their place; when harps are hung in Selma's hall; then comes a voice to Ossian, and awakes his soul! It is the voice of years that are gone! they roll before me, with all their deeds!"

"The king heard the music of harps, the tales of other times! The chiefs gathered from all their hills, and heard the lovely sound. They praised the voice of Cona! the first among a thousand bards! But age is now on my tongue; my soul has failed! I hear, at times, the ghosts of bards, and learn their pleasant song. But memory fails on my mind. I hear the call of years! They say, as they pass along, why does Ossian sing? Soon shall he lie in the narrow house, and no bard shall raise his fame! Roll on, ye dark-brown years; ye bring no joy on your course! Let the tomb open to Ossian, for his strength has failed. The sons of song are gone to rest. My voice remains, like a blast, that roars, lonely, on a sea-surrounded rock, after the winds are laid. The dark moss whistles there; the distant mariner sees the waving trees!"

A daughter alone is left to him, the widow of Oscar his son; and when "the awful faces of other times look down on him from the clouds," he tells her of the great deeds he has seen, and the mighty who have fallen.

"Such were the words of the bards, in the day of their mourning: Ossian often joined their voice; and added to their song. My soul has been mournful for Carthon; he fell in the days of his youth; and thou, O Clessámmor! where is thy dwelling in the wind? Has the youth forgot his wound? Flies he, on clouds, with thee? I feel the sun, O Malvina! leave me to my rest. Perhaps they may come to my dreams;

I think I hear a feeble voice! The beam of heaven delights to shine on the grave of Carthon: I feel it warm around!

"O thou that rollest above, round as the shield of my fathers! Whence are thy beams, O sun! thy everlasting light? Thou comest forth, in thy awful beauty; the stars hide themselves in the sky; the moon, cold and pale, sinks in the western wave. But thou thyself movest alone: who can be a companion of thy course? The oaks of the mountains fall: the mountains themselves decay with years; the ocean shrinks and grows again; the moon herself is lost in heaven; but thou art for ever the same; rejoicing in the brightness of thy course. When the world is dark with tempests; when thunder rolls, and lightning flies; thou lookest in thy beauty from the clouds, and laughest at the storm. But to Ossian thou lookest in vain; for he beholds thy beams no more; whether thy yellow hair flows on the eastern clouds, or thou tremblest at the gates of the west. But thou art perhaps, like me, for a season; thy years will have an end. Thou shalt sleep in thy clouds, careless of the voice of the morning. Exult thee, O sun! in the strength of thy youth! Age is dark and unlovely; it is like the glimmering light of the moon, when it shines through broken clouds, and the mist is on the hills; the blast of north is on the plain; the traveller shrinks in the midst of his journey."

But though his friends live again in his song, this too in the end will fade from the land like mist: "We shall pass away like a dream. No

sound will remain in our fields of war. Our
tombs will be lost in the heath ; the hunter
shall not know the place of our rest."

Such were the mournful tones of this Highland poetry, as it appeared when it was translated out of the Gaelic language, and presented
in elegant English by James Macpherson, a
young student of fair talents and unblemished
character, who had kept a school in the district
of Badenoch, in Inverness-shire, where, by his
own account, fragments of this poetry were commonly recited. He spent some of his leisure in
collecting them. By a fortunate chance they
were brought to the notice of certain distinguished men in Edinburgh, who received them
at first with astonishment, and then with delight
that poems of such manifest beauty, and, as was
proved by their simple character and the life
which they portrayed, of so great an antiquity,
should have been preserved in the unexplored
regions of their own country. The fragments
that were first published were read with enthusiasm ; and Scotchmen everywhere felt that if no
considerable writer had hitherto arisen among
them, they had in Ossian a poet who could rank
with the great masters of the ancient world.

It was in the year 1760 that this new star appeared in the northern heavens ; for more than half a century it shone with great splendour ; and though its fires have long since paled, it can still be seen by eager observers in certain latitudes.

But its size and brilliance and the matter of which it was composed were everywhere debated. The poems were hardly read by the men of letters in Edinburgh before their authenticity was suspected ; and a controversy arose which is not yet extinct. It began in a gentle form with the publication of a few random fragments ; even though in the almost unanimous opinion of the best judges there was little reason to doubt that the pieces which Macpherson produced in English were genuine specimens of rude Gaelic verse. But when he collected a large number of these waifs and strays of Highland poetry, and under the notion that he was dealing with fragments of a regular epic assigned to them all a like antiquity, and gave them a unity which perhaps they did not possess ; when he rendered them in an orderly form, and in a free and polished paraphrase, and presented the six books of *Fingal* and the

eight of *Temora* as translations of epic poems
composed by Ossian in the third century, and
handed down from mouth to mouth for fifty
generations, suspicion ripened into an open attack on the translator's honesty.   The attack
on Macpherson chiefly proceeded from London,
where suspicion was aided and inflamed by the
hatred and contempt which happened to prevail
at the time for everything connected with the
Scottish race ; and the question of the authenticity of the poems assumed an international
colour.   While their merits gained them a great
share of popular admiration, critical opinion ran
to extremes : they were either welcomed with
acclamation as a long-lost work of stupendous
genius, or else roundly denounced as bombastic
trash and a barefaced forgery.   Blair, the literary dictator of the Scottish capital, put Ossian
on a higher level than Homer ; and Johnson,
who ruled in the south, branded Macpherson
as a gross impostor.   Others, like Gray, Hume,
and Gibbon, with less ardour and more dis-
crimination, selected various features of the
poems for special criticism, of a nature sometimes favourable and sometimes adverse to their
authenticity ; but while the learned exhausted

their arguments, the poems were everywhere read.

Nor is it difficult to explain their success. When the fame of a literary work is permanent, no other explanation suffices than its own intrinsic merit : but when an author previously unknown attains an immediate popularity, we shall seldom err if we look chiefly to some external reason for the source of it. Critics [1] have declared that the Ossianic poems, in the form in which Macpherson produced them, were successful because they gave new expression to a sentimental gloom prevailing at the moment. That they are largely sentimental is not to be denied ; but it is more than doubtful whether their success can be so explained, or whether their sentiment had in it anything peculiarly akin to contemporary fashions. We associate a dreary sentimentalism with Young's *Night Thoughts*, with Robert Blair's *Grave*, and with Hervey's *Meditations;* and there is sentiment of another character in Richardson's novels, and in Sterne's *Tristram Shandy*, and gloom of a noble and stately cast in Gray's *Elegy*. *Tristram*

[1] Among others, the late Prof. Henry Morley, in his admirable *First Sketch of English Literature*, p. 862.

Shandy appeared about the same time as Macpherson's production; the *Elegy* was published ten years, and the other works fifteen or twenty years previously; but their several characteristics are entirely different from the tone and quality of the Ossianic poems. We must remember that literature is rarely free from some kind of sentimentalism, and that, wherever it is found, it is often merely a vicious outcome of that feeling for the pathos of life which gives to all poetry its best and perennial inspiration. Instead of owing their success to the prevalence of a morbid feeling, it is rather the case that the Ossianic poems, by their peculiar melancholy, were themselves a chief agent in the spread of sentimentalism in Europe.

The interest in the poems was at first purely external; it was bound up with interest in the Highlands; and the chapter of accidents which led to the success of *Fingal* and *Temora* began in the Jacobite rising. When the insurgent clans marched to Derby in 1745 there was a panic in London: but the alarm of that year quickly yielded to a feeling of curiosity; and although curiosity was mixed with the kind of bitter contempt which is often born of previous shame, it was not on that account less real. Those who had travelled in the north of Scotland wrote and spoke of it as of a newly discovered country, and descriptions were eagerly read. Burt's famous *Letters,* written at an earlier date, appeared in 1754; and they formed a very effective and welcome account of the natural features of the Highlands, and the strange manners, customs, and superstitions of the inhabitants. When it was rumoured that in the same neglected region there was ancient poetry of extraordinary merit, which had already been received with delight in literary circles in Edinburgh, expectation ran high; and to enhance the interest with which this wonderful product of the mountains was awaited, there was the rumour that it was too wonderful to be authentic. The feeling of curiosity remained for a long time unabated. Many years later, when Johnson went to the Hebrides, he satisfied a popular demand in issuing the journal of his tour; and not until Scott published his lays and novels did the Highlands become familiar ground, and a new interest in them arise which eclipsed the popularity of Macpherson's production.

The scenery of the poems was a source of delight new to the taste of the time. In some measure the way had been prepared for it by the love of simple nature, which in spite of the dominant influence of Pope had already shown itself in the literature of the earlier part of the century; nor is it unworthy of notice in this connection that the first long poem devoted to the pleasures and emotions of rural life was the work of a Scotchman. In Thomson's *Seasons* this feeling found ample, if somewhat stilted, expression; it was continued in the pure verse of John Dyer, who depicted the finer and gentler features of Welsh landscape; in Shenstone and Akenside it was mingled with curious affectations or the moral doctrines of contemporary philosophers; and in Collins and Gray, nature, though reflected in some of its quiet moods with great tenderness and beauty, became not so much the inspiration as the graceful ornament of poetry. But in the works of these writers it was the more familiar aspects of country life that were drawn, and the noise and the crime of the city were contrasted with an artless innocence that dwelt in fields and woods. The Ossianic poems were conceived in a grander vein. They opened a wide view of

a rugged landscape, of lake and mountain, of
streams roaring down narrow valleys, and vacant
heaths swept by wind and rain. As in almost all
the earlier poetry that came from Scotland, the
colours were intense and sharply distinguished;
a few bold strokes sufficed for description; the
imagery was of the rudest and most direct character, and the general effect was heightened
by a forced and abrupt style. Later poets
have given us purer and gentler tones; but
to readers weary of the arid conventionalities
of Pope and his school, Macpherson's work
presented a striking and impressive picture.
Some of its description appears to us now to be
cheap and tawdry, but many passages of en-
during beauty remain. Nature in its varying
appearance is made to reflect and illustrate human
emotion in a way elsewhere unparalleled; and
the heroic figures in the scene are clothed with
something of its melancholy grandeur.

Hitherto, a mountainous land was, in the
common opinion, a region of terror, where everything was harsh and repulsive. There were men
who could describe the beauties of quiet scenery
with rapture, and yet were appalled by a rugged
landscape. In no other writer of the time is the

contrast between the love of smiling plains and
the dislike of wild nature so instructive as in
Goldsmith, who was indifferent to the Highlands
because, as he said, hills and rocks intercepted
every prospect.   A like sentiment oppressed
him when he travelled in the Alps—

" Where the bleak Swiss their stormy mansion
        tread
  And force a churlish soil for scanty bread.
  No product here the barren hills afford. . . .
  No zephyr fondly sues the mountain's breast,
  But meteors glare and stormy glooms invest."

It is the feeling of solitude, with a touch,
perhaps, of the old terror still haunting it, that
gives a rugged landscape the special character
which, by an extension of the original meaning
of the word, we now describe as romantic.   Solitude and terror, deprived of their dangers and
seen from a distance, have become sublime.
This fresh spring of poetic emotion was first
opened in English literature in the Ossianic
poems ; and, whatever may be their origin or
their history, if they had no other claim to importance, they would deserve it on that ground.
They show the earliest beginnings of that attitude to nature, doubtless full of fallacy, but

adding immeasurably to the pathos of human life, which Byron has so finely described.

" I live not in myself, but I become
  Portion of that around me ; and to me
  High mountains are a feeling, and the hum
  Of human cities torture : I can see
  Nothing to loathe in nature, save to be
  A link reluctant in a fleshly chain,
  Classed among creatures, when the soul can flee,
  And with the sky, the peak, the heaving plain
  Of ocean, or the stars, mingle and not in vain."

The antiquity assigned to the work was another element in its charm. A few years previously Gray had shown in *The Bard,* and in the odes which he wrote in imitation of Norse and Welsh ballads, that simple tales from a rude age had an interest of their own ; and this tendency to look to the past for the materials of poetry helped in a high degree to form the character of the romantic spirit. It is everywhere present in the Ossianic poems ; and a further and more effective illustration of it appeared in 1765, in the *Reliques of Ancient English Poetry,* collected and edited by Percy. The men and women in these old Highland songs were presented as vague figures moving on the dim horizon of Scottish history, lost as it were in

the night of time; and a strange pathos surrounded the blind singer in an antique age
who bewailed his fate as the last of a race of
heroes.

This new combination of sentimentalism with
a love for wild scenery and an interest in the
past aroused an astonishing enthusiasm. Although many other influences were at work in
forming the ideas and directing the sympathies
of the romantic movement when it was gathering
strength in the later years of the eighteenth
century, the Ossianic poems, which were widely
read abroad and freely translated, rapidly became
a leading force in changing the popular taste.
In Italy the fresh ideas which they embodied
found an ardent champion in the Abbé Cesarotti,
a writer of some authority at the time, who
declared that amongst his own acquaintances
they had produced a new school of poetic composition.   In Germany they gave a vigorous
impulse to the movement known as the *Sturm
und Drang*. They were greeted with ecstasy,
and everywhere reflected; Herder was foremost
in praising them as a magnificent discovery;
Bürger turned some of them into verse; Klop-
stock and his friends hastened to write their

in a work which had delighted him as a youth. In 1793 Coleridge wrote two poems expressly described as imitations of Ossian.   Byron in his *Hours of Idleness* shows unmistakable touches of Ossianic sentiment, as in the verses on Oscar of Alva, and sometimes a reminiscence of the Ossianic language ; and he wrote a passage in prose entitled *The Death of Calmar and Orla,* in which he himself attempted the Ossianic vein.   To this he appended a note in which he expressed his boyish opinion, that although it might be proved that Macpherson's work was not a translation of poems complete in themselves, its merit remained undisputed, in spite of its turgid diction ; and he offered his humble imitation to the admirers of the original as a proof of his attachment to their favourite author.   Wordsworth, it need hardly be said, wrote of the poems with undisguised contempt. He applied an over-subtle canon of natural description to their imagery, and denounced it as spurious ; and thus he claimed to have discovered an irrefragable proof that they were unworthy of their wide reputation.[1]   Scott in his early years had a fair share of the Ossianic fever ; but,

---

[1] *The Excursion :* Essay supplementary to the Preface.

as he shows in one of the most lively chapters of *The Antiquary*, his mature opinion was equally unfavourable to the merits of the poems and to their authenticity. However, in spite of criticism and abuse, they long kept their position; and even a writer with the insight of Elizabeth Barrett Browning found a place for the grey old bard in her *Vision of Poets :—*

> " . . . Ossian, dimly seen or guessed,
>   Once counted greater than the rest,
>   When mountain-winds blew out his vest ".

Such, in briefest outline, was the influence of these poems on the literature of Europe. From the beginning an air of mystery has surrounded their origin; and now, when they are no longer read, and their prodigious effect is forgotten, it is the common belief that they were a bubble blown by James Macpherson. This belief is in a very large measure an intellectual inheritance which we have received from Johnson; as he now occupies a great, and Macpherson a very small, position in the annals of our literature, his authority on the subject still prevails. Thus it is that most Englishmen are guided by the opinion which he roundly expressed as to the merits of Macpherson's work; though, in truth, there was no one less competent by the nature of his literary sympathies to form a just opinion. In the same way most Englishmen derive their idea of Macpherson himself from the odious light in which he stands in Boswell's pages. He is there pilloried as an insolent forger, who, when he failed to convince the sage, threatened him with personal violence, and received at his hands no better treatment than he deserved. The rights and the wrongs of the famous quarrel between them are decided by recollections of an abusive letter which Johnson addressed to his antagonist, who, by Boswell's art, is made, and unfairly made, to appear as the aggressor. Every one reads Boswell's *Life of Johnson;* but there are very few who know anything of Macpherson's real character, or of the circumstances in which he produced his work, or of the nature of the attack that was made upon it.

The aim of the following narrative is to throw some light upon these matters. If Macpherson was merely an editor and translator of Gaelic fragments, he is an interesting figure ; for out of rough materials he composed a work that not only enjoyed an enormous success in this country, but also exercised an immediate and profound influence abroad, to which the previous history of our literature offered no parallel ; if he was himself the author of the work, he is not less, but still more, interesting. He was for several years the centre of a controversy remarkable for its popularity, for the eminence of those who were engaged in it, and for an extraordinary display of prejudice ; and where so much depends on the honesty or dishonesty of the alleged translator, it is expedient to show, by the recovery of every scrap of evidence now available, what manner of man he was, and how he proceeded in his task.

CHAPTER II.

The Macphersons.—Birth.—Ruthven, and the
Rising of '45.—Education at Aberdeen.—
Return to Ruthven as Schoolmaster.—
Early Poetry.

The biography of any man fitly begins with the
mention of his ancestors. To know something
of the race of which he came not only gratifies
a reasonable curiosity ; but it helps or ought to
help us in forming a right estimate of what he
was in himself; and this is all the more needful
if any uncertainty attaches to his doings. His
race, it may be said, is the long shadowy prelude
to the drama of his individual life ; and in the
course of nature his part is, in some measure at
least, determined for him there before he enters.
As we watch him, mostly an ill-defined figure,
strut his little hour upon the stage, and in the
twilight of the past do what we can to follow
him through the scenes of his history, it may
be useful to remember the character of the
prelude ; it may sometimes assist a just under-

standing of his action at critical moments in his career.

The Macphersons are an important clan in the Highlands of Scotland, mainly inhabiting the southern parts of the county of Inverness, and, in particular, the district of Badenoch. They form one of the two principal branches of the ancient clan Chattan. One had need to be a Highlander to take a proper interest in the conflicting accounts that have been given of the origin of this clan, or to describe its fortunes with adequate enthusiasm. In sober prose its members are the reputed descendants of one Gillicattan, who, as the name implies, was a votary or servant of St. Kattan, a Scottish saint ; but some deny that they were native Celts and make them foreign adventurers, of the German tribe of the Catti or Hessians, mentioned by Tacitus. The Celtic name of the Macphersons is Mac Mhuirich. This they are said to have obtained from one Mhuirich or Murdoch, who in 1153 was parson of Kingussie, a religious colony in lower Badenoch, founded by Irish missionaries at a much earlier date. Upon the death of his elder brother without issue, Mhuirich succeeded to the chiefship of the

clan, and obtaining a dispensation from the
Pope, he married a daughter of the Thane of
Cawdor and became the father of five sons. It
was from this office of "parson" that his heirs
obtained the surname of Macpherson, properly
Macphersain. Their history, like that of most
clans in the Highlands, is a long record of feuds
with other clans. They were often at open war
with the Mackintoshes, the rival branch of their
own sept, in the bitter struggle for supremacy :
a struggle carried on at first by the sword, and
then at law, and even still in our own day
waged with the pen. Their disputes led them
into antagonism with the Camerons and the
Davidsons, and between them all there was
continual strife and enmity. They were ardent
supporters of Queen Mary in the sixteenth and
Charles the First in the seventeenth century.
They took a leading part in resisting the Earl of
Argyle when he marched with a royalist army
against the Earls of Huntly and Errol and other
Catholics in 1594 ; and their chief, John Macpherson, stoutly and successfully defended the
Castle of Ruthven in Badenoch, and afterwards
fought under Huntly at the battle of Glenlivet.
They led a rough and lawless life ; the Highlands

were then, and indeed for long afterwards, in a
condition little removed from savagery ; most
of the inhabitants had no intercourse with the
outer world ; and from the character of their
country, a wild mountainous district with here
and there a rude path, they had little means of
communication even amongst themselves.

At the time of the great Civil War the chief
of the clan was Donald Macpherson of Cluny,
who with his three brothers, Andrew, Lachlan
and John, fought on the royalist side and suffered
for their allegiance.   Andrew Macpherson succeeded to the chiefship in 1647.   It is set down
to his credit that of his own free will he assisted
the rival branch of the clan in an expedition
against the Camerons ; but in return for his
services he shrewdly demanded that a deed
should be executed, binding Mackintosh to assist
him and his brothers in such lawful action as
they might be compelled to undertake.   In 1672
Andrew was succeeded by his grandson Duncan,
whose title to fame is an attempt which he made
to have his arms entered on the roll of the Lyon
office, as the only true representative of the clan.
The Mackintoshes, enraged at this attack on their
supremacy, appealed to the Privy Council ; and

the Council, recognising each branch as independent, bound over the chiefs for the peaceable behaviour of their followers—a decision which was
regarded by the Macphersons as a victory. Duncan died without issue in 1722, and was succeeded
by Lachlan Macpherson, a descendant of John of
Nuid, the youngest brother of the chiefs Donald
and Andrew.[1]

Such were the men of whom James Macpherson came ; and if most of them found their
distinction more in the arts of war than in the
arts of peace, their harsh life, while it made
them rough, made them also a proud, sensitive,
and spirited race. It was to William, the second
son of this same John of Nuid, that he traced
his descent. In an account published when he
was at the height of his reputation, and probably
written by one of his friends, it was stated that
he was a cousin to the chief of the clan ; and
the statement was no more than the truth.
His family is there described, with a pardonable
flourish, as one of the most ancient in the
north of Scotland. Macpherson's parents, however, were not able to hold their heads very

---

[1] See Keltie's *History of the Scottish Highlands*, ii. 211 ;
and Wm. Anderson's *The Scottish Nation*, iii. 60-66.

high. Of his father, Andrew Macpherson, all
that is known is that he was a poor farmer
in Ruthven, a village a little to the south of
Kingussie, on the other side of the river Spey.
It was there that young Macpherson was born
and brought up, "a barefit laddie". His mother,
by name Ellen, was also a Macpherson, of another and obscurer branch of the family ; and her
father, a tacksman, that is, holder of a tack or
lease, seems to have been in much the same
position as her husband. We learn that Macpherson had sisters ;[1] but if he had any brothers,
nothing is known of them.

The conflict of evidence which almost everywhere marks our knowledge of Macpherson's
career makes an early and appropriate beginning
over the date of his birth. Until recently, in all
encyclopædias, dictionaries of biography, and wherever else a sketch of his life is attempted, his birth
has been assigned to the latter end of the year
1738, and that is the date given in the account

---

[1] Janet and Margaret. One of them married a Mr. Clark
of Invernahaven, and to their son the late Sir John Macdonald, Premier of Canada, was related by marriage. See
Glimpses of Church and Social Life in the Highlands, an
interesting volume by Mr. Alex. Macpherson, to which I am
indebted for one or two facts mentioned in this chapter.

published in his lifetime. A man's own testimony is generally accepted as to the date of his birth;[1] but if he comes of a humble family in a remote district long unvisited, he may easily be mistaken as to the exact year of that event. Among the various charges brought against Macpherson, no one accused him of falsifying his age; and yet if he had been born towards the end of the year 1738 his early achievements would be rendered still more remarkable than they are. None, apparently, of those who have hitherto described his career thought it worth while to visit the spot where it ended,—his grave in Westminster Abbey. The inscription thereon states that he was born on the 27th of October, 1736; and as it would presumably have been ordered by some intimate friend or relative, its testimony would in itself be of great value. But it is satisfactory to know that there still exists

[1] In the preface to the fourth edition of *Fingal* (1773) Macpherson declared that he was twenty-four years of age when the first edition appeared, in 1762; and according to that declaration he would have been born in 1738. But it is strange that all those who adopt this date say that when he died, in February, 1796, he was in his fifty-ninth year, and the discrepancy has hitherto passed unobserved. He was, in fact, fifty-nine years old when he died.

in the possession of his descendants an important document giving the same date.[1]

Macpherson's birthplace, Ruthven, is a village on the north side of the Grampians, about half way on the great Highland road between Perth and Inverness. It is a village of some antiquity; and that it was anciently celebrated is probable from the fact that it is one of the very few places in the far North which Ptolemy (A.D. 140) mentions in his account of Britain. In the neighbourhood may be found the remains of Druidical circles and the vestiges of a Roman camp; and it is said that a Roman vase was once discovered there. The old monastery of the parish had long disappeared even in Macpherson's time; but enthusiastic antiquaries, not a great many years ago, pointed out the ruins of it, or at least of some ancient building devoted to religious uses.

[1] In Nicholls' *Literary Anecdotes*, ix. 525, the date on the tomb is, by a curious mistake, given as 3rd July, 1728. The document now in the possession of Mr. Brewster Macpherson is a memo   nt by a notary at Ruthven to one of Macpherson   rs, the minister at Kingussie; and in view of the   the document is addressed to his executor in the wing that of his death, it is fair to conclude that ation which it supplies is the source of the date the tomb in the Abbey, and that this date is corre

These remnants of the past would be likely to have had an influence on the mind of a boy with any vein of romance in him; but they had no conspicuous effect on Macpherson, so far, at least, as we can judge by his youthful efforts in poetry. On the other hand, we can gather from the same source of information that at an early age he learnt to admire the scenery surrounding his home, after a fashion rare with those who are brought up to hard work in a mountainous district. To the poor farmer and his children nature showed as harsh a face as the world; and the feeling for fine scenery quickly yielded to the stern necessity of making a living.

" In Donald's eye now fade the blissful scenes—
The rough-browed rocks, the sloping hills and
    plains,
Delight no more; no chase, no wingèd fowl,
No goat, no cattle, cheer the troubled soul;
The hut is hateful, and the fields of corn
Contract their bounds and promise no return.
All is one blank—O envy'd, envy'd state,
The hunter cries, of all the happy great!
While press'd in poverty's hard iron hand,
I force poor sustenance from barren land,
Remote from life and curs'd by fate unkind
To struggle on the hill with northern wind.
. . . The hut, the heathy wild, the barren fold,
The rattling hail, the north-descended cold
Is all my portion." [1]

        [1] *The Hunter*, canto ii.

There are no anecdotes reported of Macpherson's boyhood to derive their interest from his subsequent celebrity, nor is there any account of his early education, except that it began at home; from which it may be inferred that his parents, although in a poor position, possessed a fair measure of instruction. Even in the wildest part of the Highlands this would scarcely serve to mark them off from their neighbours of the same class. For, thanks to the efforts of the Roman Church in an earlier century, and more particularly to the excellent system of Protestant parochial schools established soon after the Revolution, the elements of education were at that time more widely diffused in Scotland than in any other part of the British Isles. When he could learn no more from his parents, young Macpherson was sent to the parochial school. There he gave so much evidence of talent that his father, contrary, it is said, to his original intention, determined to bring him up to a learned profession. The Highland farmer's idea of a learned profession did not soar beyond the Church : to make his son a minister would make him a scholar, if not a gentleman ; and accordingly it was with a view to entry into

the ministry that young Macpherson thenceforth
received the best education that could be obtained for him. One authority states that he
remained on in the parochial school in Badenoch
until he proceeded to college; another, that he
spent some time previously at the grammar
school in Inverness.

An event happened in his early years which
cannot fail to have excited his imagination. At
the age of nine, when most boys are playing at
soldiers, Macpherson saw something of the effects
of real war at his father's doors, in the rising of
'45. The site of the Castle of Ruthven, the
ancient seat of the Comyns, lords of Badenoch,
had been for some thirty years occupied by barracks, where troops were stationed to overawe
the inhabitants of that district. But the soldiers
had little to do, and they and their followers
were often the cause of scandal to the respectable villagers. In 1745 the greater part of the
garrison accompanied Sir John Cope on his
march to Prestonpans, leaving one sergeant in
charge with twelve men. Thereupon two hundred of the population attacked the barracks;
but it was only in the following year that the
small garrison was compelled to surrender to

an assault of some three hundred more, under
Gordon of Glenbucket. The Macphersons, who
were eager adherents of the old Pretender in
1715, joined the rising in 1745 apparently out
of a desire to avenge the death of three of the
clansmen who had been shot after the mutiny
of the Black Watch, afterwards the 42nd regiment, two years previously. The chief of the
clan, Ewen Macpherson of Cluny, had taken
the oaths to Government before Prince Charles'
arrival, and had accepted a commission in a
Highland regiment; but, urged by his clan, he
threw it up, and with six hundred of his name
joined the insurgents after their first victory.
The Macphersons accompanied Prince Charles
on his march into England, and showed great
gallantry whenever they were engaged; but they
arrived too late to share in the defeat at Culloden,
or else, as was maintained at the time, to turn
the fortune of the day. In the subsequent opera-
tions of the English army, Cluny's house was
plundered and burnt; his estates were forfeited;
and although a price was set upon his head, by
the devotion of his clan he succeeded, as is well
known, in hiding himself for many years before
he escaped to France. Cluny's house was not

far distant from Ruthven, and young Macpherson
will have been an actual witness of many of the
smaller incidents of the fray, especially as the
fighting men of the clan were quartered in Ruthven itself; and it was there that the Pretender's
followers assembled after their defeat. To save
the barracks from capture by the Royalists, they
were burnt; and the walls alone are now standing. The effects of these exciting scenes may
perhaps be traced in the martial character of
Macpherson's early poems; but the stormy sentiments which they aroused found long afterwards
a serious expression in his political writings.

Towards the end of the year 1752, at the age
of sixteen, he prepared to enter King's College,
Aberdeen, or, as it was then styled, "the University and King's College of Aberdeen". Although
his name, "Jacobus Macpherson, Invernensis,"
does not appear on the matriculation roll until
February, 1753, it is said by John Ramsay[1] that

[1] Ramsay of Ochtertyre (1736-1814) is well known as
the patron of Burns and the friend of Scott. He took
voluminous notes of men and events in the last quarter of
the eighteenth century; and in 1888 a selection from them
was published under the title of *Scotland and Scotsmen of
the Eighteenth Century.* Vol. i., p. 545, contains an interesting account of Macpherson.

he entered in the previous November, and that, in common with most of those who were destined for the ministry, he obtained a bursarship.   Of his career at college it is not recorded that it was in any way remarkable.   The university at the time could boast of the presence of Thomas Reid, the philosopher, as the most conspicuous orna- ment of the professorial body ; but Macpherson, then and afterwards, showed no inclination to philosophy.   By all accounts it is probable that he neglected the special opportunities of the place ; for in the opinion of the authorities he is said to have displayed more genius than learning. It is easy to see what was meant by this state- ment, particularly as he was then making various efforts to write poetry.   Most idle students, nay most students when they are idle, do the same. To a boy fresh from the wildest districts of the Highlands mere existence in Aberdeen must have been an education in itself, more attrac- tive and in its effect more stimulating than any course of collegiate studies ; for in the extreme north at that period of Scottish history, Aber- deen was the one centre of civilisation.   But we learn that Macpherson read widely, and made himself a fair classical scholar ; and, by the admission of those who afterwards attacked him, he obtained an extensive acquaintance with modern literature.

If we may judge by the solitary story[1] that is told of his college-days, it is hardly likely that he was popular with his fellow-students. He had a standing feud with a very poor, ugly and awkward lad, named Machardy, who was with him in the Greek class ; and on one occasion he mocked him in some lines of Hudibrastic verse. Machardy, picking up courage, retorted in heroics, and turned the laugh against Macpherson. The quarrel was coming to extremities when it was brought to the notice of the professor, the learned Dr. Blackwell, principal of the college. He ordered both culprits to produce their effusions, and read them with much gravity to the whole class. After making some severe comments on their literary failings, he ordered both writers to keep the peace, under pain of expulsion. Macpherson, it is said, was very indignant.

He took no degree from King's College ; it is doubtful whether he remained there long enough to enable him to take a degree. In the

---

[1] *Scotland and Scotsmen of the Eighteenth Century.*

year 1755 the authorities resolved to add two
months to the length of the annual session; a
proceeding which bore hard upon the poorer
students, many of whom were sons of farmers.
Then as now, poor students in a Scotch university were compelled to spend the summer months
in earning enough to pay for their classes in the
winter.   But in the new part of the town and
side by side with King's College in the old part,
there was Marischal College, which at that time
was not only a separate institution but formed a
university by itself.   Education there was somewhat cheaper, as no addition was made to its session; and thither, accordingly, many of the poorer
students migrated, Macpherson amongst them.

On leaving Marischal College he went to
the University of Edinburgh.   His name does
not appear in the matriculation album; and it
is therefore clear that he did not enter that
university as a student of arts, or of law or
medicine; but there is some possibility that
students of divinity alone, especially if they
came from another university, were not then
required to matriculate.[1]   It was probably in

[1] The suggestion is kindly furnished by the registrar of
the university.

the winter of 1755-6 that he was in Edinburgh; for in the following winter we find him back again in Ruthven, and writing a brief and unfavourable description of the city.

Macpherson was still too young to enter the ministry, and he returned to Ruthven to look about him for the means of making a livelihood. He was hardly twenty; and, for want of something better to do, he took over the charity school in his native village, where he had already managed to earn a little money during his vacation. As it was the only school in the whole district from Speymouth to Lorne, the position was not undistinguished. The employment left him plenty of leisure, and it was then that he wrote most of his early poems. His first attempts were not published, and they would probably never have seen the light if the manuscript of two of them had not come into the hands of his most energetic opponent, who printed them for a controversial purpose, just in the condition in which they were found That Macpherson never intended, perhaps never wished, to publish them is probable from the fact that they were found in their first rough draft, stitched together into the form of a small note-book. That they

were written at this time appears by some
memoranda on one of the leaves relating to his
school and housekeeping; and to one of the
passages the date of its composition is affixed.

There is not much to be said for these
poems. They are on the same level as the productions of most young students with a literary
ambition; they are no good; in parts they
are even ludicrous. One of them, in blank verse,
is apparently an imitation of Robert Blair's
Grave, which was published in 1743. It is
entitled *Death*; and although it contains a few
fair similes, it is certainly a dreary performance.
The other is an unnamed effort in heroics, and
in ten cantos, to which one of Macpherson's
critics gave the name of *The Hunter,* to distinguish it from a later production, somewhat
resembling it, *The Highlander.* The following
passages show the kind of original work of
which Macpherson was capable at the age of
twenty; and they are selected, not because of
any peculiar merit, for of that they have little,
but as showing their author's early liking for
descriptions of battle, and the character of his
feeling for nature. In *The Hunter* the influence
of Thomson's *Seasons* is sufficiently obvious; but

it will be observed that the imagery is in
thorough accord with the prevailing style of
the time; for it betrays the study of classical
models rather than any capacity for direct observation.

> " Whether the sun sports in the fields of light,
>   Or gloomy night her sable mantle throws
> O'er sleeping earth, still imaged to the mind
> Of young Andræmon is his darling friend.
> Still sighs the breast, still melts the tearful eye,
> Still flows the soul in elegies of woe.
> The rocks, the plains, the woods, the pleasing
>   scenes
> Where he and young Philætes, raptured, prayed
> And talked of virtue, echo to his moan.
> Sleep'st thou for ever, O my darling friend !
> . . . He said—'twas night, and solemn silence
>   reigned
> Throughout the plain ; no voice, no sound is
>   heard,
> But now and then the breathing breezes sigh
> Through the half-quivering leaves, and, far
>   removed,
> The sea rolls feeble murmurs to the shore."

This is the end of the poem on *Death.* It is
neither better nor worse than the rest of it.
Macpherson was fond of night pieces, and
attempts several of them in his *Hunter*.

> " Thus in the horizon of the silent night
>   The setting moon darts parallel its light,
>   Silvers the flood and paints the landscape gay,

And deals around the bright nocturnal day :
But sunk beneath, the pleasing prospects fail,
And every object wears a melancholy veil.
Sunk in a flood of heart-corroding woes
O'erwhelm'd I stood ; another scene arose."

In every canto of this poem we come upon
the clash of arms.

" Death undetermined points to each his sting,
And conquest flutters round on dubious wing,
The hill-born youth reminds, with anxious
    care,
What vaunts the foul-mouth'd Saxon breathed
    on air ;
His country's love the youthful hero warms,
And vengeance strung his almost wearied arms.
Upraised aloft the light reflexive blade
Sings through the air, and cleaves the Saxon's
    head.
The broken skull and shiver'd helmet strew'd
The sandy plain, that reeks with human blood.
He gasping falls and shakes the thundering
    ground,
And dying toss'd his quivering limbs around.
Thus falls an oak that long majestic stood
The tallest honours of the waving wood ;
Deep hack'd by the shipwright's unerring hand,
Groans, slow inclines, and falling shakes the
    land."

There was undoubtedly much room for
improvement in these effusions, and some of it
was marked in *The Highlander*, which found a
publisher in Edinburgh about a year and a half

later, in April, 1758 Opinions differ as to its reception. An anonymous critic in a magazine described it as "a tissue of fustian and absurdity"; and it is generally said of it that it fell dead from the press. The publisher, Ruddiman, writing sixteen years afterwards, when Macpherson was famous, affirmed that it had a very rapid sale. Whatever Ruddiman's statement may be worth, it is undeniable that Macpherson, obscure before this work was published, was equally obscure after it. It is also said that he was conscious himself of the defects of the poem, and tried to suppress it; but if *The Highlander* was ever possessed of any vitality, there was hardly enough of it to need suppression. It is in six cantos, and also in the heroic strain. Its subject appears to be the invasion of Scotland by the Danes in the reign of Malcolm II. in the eleventh century, and it gave Macpherson full scope for the treatment of his favourite topics. It abounds in combats. A fair specimen of its general style is afforded by the opening lines of canto iii.

"As when beneath the night's tempestuous
    cloud,
  Embattled winds assail the leafy wood,

Tear on their sable way with awful sound,
And bring the groaning forest to the ground :
The trunks of elms, the shrub, the fir, the oak
In one confusion sink beneath the shock :
So death's sad spoils the bloody field be-
    strow'd ;
The haughty chieftain, the ignoble crowd,
The coward, brave, partake the common
    wound,
Are friends in death, and mingle on the ground.
  Dark night approach'd : the flaming lord
    of day
Had plunged his glowing circle in the sea ;
On the blue sky the gath'ring clouds arise,
And tempests clap their wings along the skies ;
The murm'ring voice of heaven, at distance,
    fails,
And eddying whirlwinds howl along the vales."

About this time Macpherson began to send poetical pieces to the *Scots Magazine.* This was then the only literary periodical published north of the Tweed, and in the twenty years of its existence, it had obtained no small popularity. His earliest contribution was a short poem, *On the Death of Marshal Keith.* James Keith, who, with his more celebrated brother George, commonly known as the Earl Marischal, was a Jacobite refugee, had served in various foreign armies, and at his death on the 14th of October, 1758, was a field-marshal of Prussia. His memory was widely cherished, and Macpherson did no more than express the admiration which Scotchmen everywhere felt for the man who had carried the name and fame of their country to the uttermost ends of Europe. Mingled with this pride there was an undertone of the Jacobite sentiment still prevailing in many parts of the Highlands, and ready to respond to anything that called it forth. Macpherson's poem was written from Ruthven before the end of October; and this shows us that the news of Keith's death spread very rapidly. Two more pieces bearing Macpherson's initials appeared in the following year. In one of them he bewailed the death of a young lady, "the last but fairest of a falling name," with whom he had been, as his lines show, on terms of intimate friendship; in the other he commemorated the loss of an officer, also a close friend, who had been killed in the storming of Quebec. Whether we regard the ease of the verse or the nature of the feeling which they exhibit, these short poems are far superior to any of Macpherson's earlier efforts.[1]

[1] The lines *On the Death of Marshal Keith* appeared without Macpherson's name or initials in a "*Collection of*

4

It was the ambition of this obscure young schoolmaster to succeed as an original poet. In

Original Poems by the Rev. Mr. Blacklock and other Scots Gentlemen," vol. i., published in Edinburgh, in 1760. They were doubtless inserted because of their subject, and perhaps also in order to include something by a man who had just then won his literary spurs. The poem was placed last in the Collection, with an editorial note ; and this circumstance makes it probable that none of the other anonymous pieces in that volume came from the same author. Yet Malcolm Laing (*Poems of Ossian*, ii. 601, Edinburgh, 1805), who was very anxious to show how much original poetry Macpherson had written before he produced *Fingal* and *Temora*, had no hesitation in ascribing to Macpherson, and reprinting as his, a series of fifteen poems in that volume for which no other author could be found. They consist of translations from Horace, Tyrtæus and Anacreon, together with one or two other pieces in the ordinary strain of the elegant versifier. There is only one of them, a ballad called *The Cave*, which is of any merit; and just because of its merit, Laing was eager to claim it for the alleged translator of the Ossianic poems. But the only evidence which he offered is a slight verbal parallel between two or three detached lines of it and certain passages in *Death* and *The Hunter*. The words and expressions on which he relied, *e.g.*, " columns of smoke," " a fragment falls," are far too trite to warrant a conclusion which is entirely unsupported by the general style and sentiment of the ballad compared with the style and sentiment of Macpherson's acknowledged poems. The evidence which Laing offered for the authorship of the other pieces is of a similar character, and may be similarly refuted. None of these productions appeared in the small posthumous volume of Macpherson's poetical works, published, with a memoir, in 1802.

the words in which he spoke of these efforts
later on, he served his apprenticeship to the
muses.[1] But, as often happens in the history of
literature, nay, in every kind of history, the gifts
which fortune had in store for him lay to a very
small extent in the direction of what he supposed
to be his best capacities. He was baulked of
his particular ambition, but he obtained a bril-
liant success in another sphere, unexpected, and
greater than the wildest dreams of his youth
had ever conceived. And he found a way to it
not through his regular employment, but in the
casual amusement of his hours of leisure.

[1] Preface to *Fingal*, 4th edit., 1773.

CHAPTER III.

The *Scots Magazine* is likely to have attracted Macpherson long before he wrote anything in it himself; for the literary aspirant looks with a fond eye on the literary periodical. It would be interesting if we could show that he read it during the winter of 1755-6, which, as it seems, he spent in Edinburgh; for during that winter there appeared in its pages an English version of a Gaelic poem. It deserved attention as the first that had ever been published.

The poem was accompanied by a remarkable letter calling attention to the great quantity of Gaelic verse to be found in the Highlands. That such compositions existed was, said the writer, a fact well known to any one who had a tolerable acquaintance with Gaelic. it were not for the neglect, or rather, the abhorrence which had overtaken that emphatic language, their merit would be at once recognised. Some of them were of a high antiquity, and for sublime sentiment, nervousness of expression and high-spirited metaphor, were hardly to be equalled among the chief productions of modern times; others, again, were very tender, simple and affecting. Of the simpler sort the writer enclosed a specimen; the burden of it was, he said, not unlike Homer's story of Bellerophon, and it might gratify the curiosity of the learned to see the different treatment of the same theme by a Highland bard.

The writer of this letter was Jerome Stone, a young man who held the humble post of master of the grammar school at Dunkeld. He has a claim to be mentioned here because he was the first translator of Gaelic poetry, and the immediate forerunner of Macpherson. His history is a strange one. The son of a sailor, he was born in 1727, at Scoonie, in Fifeshire, a district in which Gaelic was then almost unknown. As a mere boy he was sent out as a pedlar with a box of braces and buttons, but he seized an early opportunity of exchanging his stock for a parcel of books. He picked up what education he could, worked his way into St. Andrews University, and took a degree there in 1750. In the meantime he had managed to learn Hebrew from a psalter in that language, and such instruction as was freely given him by the ministers whom he visited. On obtaining the post at Dunkeld, on the borders of the High-lands, he exerted himself to learn Gaelic, or, as he called it, Irish, so as to understand the lan-guage spoken by most of those amongst whom he was settled; and he took an interest in col-lecting its ancient poetry. Stone was undoubtedly capable of great things; but he died of a fever at the age of twenty-nine, only a short time after his contribution to the *Scots Magazine.*

The poem which he published, *Albin and the daughter of Mey*, was an extremely free render-ing of the original. Unfortunately, he did not publish the Gaelic copy; but, together with other poems, it was afterwards discovered among his papers.[1] As Stone's venture must at some time

---

[1] Soon after his death they were purchased at a sale in London by Mr. George Chalmers, the antiquary. Prof. Mackinnon, of Edinburgh, has since printed them, with a memoir of Stone, in the *Transactions of the Gaelic Society of Inverness*, 1887-8.

or other have come in Macpherson's way, it
will be interesting to show the kind of rendering
for which he won acceptance, if only to give an
example of the freedom which was commonly
allowed in the process of translation at that
period. The fact that Stone's version passed
for a fair one has an important bearing on any
estimate that may be formed of Macpherson's
work. The poem in the Gaelic original is entitled
Fraoch's Death; and, literally translated, the first
three verses run as follow :—[1]

" The sigh of a friend in the grove of Fraoch !
  A sigh for the hero in its rounded pale,
  A sigh which causes each man to mourn,
  And which makes each maiden weep.

" There to the westward is the cairn
  Which covers Fraoch, son of Fiach, of the soft
    hair,
  He who obeyed the call of Mey,
  And from whom that cairn of Fraoch has its
    name.

" The maids from Cruchan weep,
  Sad is the cause of their woe,
  For their mournful sighs are occasioned
  By Fraoch, son of Fiach, of the ancient weap-
    ons."

[1] They are given in the *Report of the Committee of the
Highland Society on the Poems of Ossian* (Edinb., 1805),
App., 103.

In Stone's rendering the three verses become one, and the metre is entirely altered :—

" Whence come these dismal sounds that fill our
        ears ?
    Why do the groves such lamentations send ?
    Why sit the virgins on the hill of tears,
        While heavy sighs their tender bosoms rend ?
    They weep for Albin with the flowing hair
        Who perish'd by the cruelty of Mey,
    A blameless hero, blooming, young, and fair,
        Because he scorn'd her passions to obey.
    See on yon western hill the heap of stones
        Which mourning friends have raised o'er his
        bones."

In speaking of the abhorrence which had overtaken the Gaelic language, Stone used an expression which was none too strong. The English Government had for some time been doing its utmost to suppress the language altogether. It was partly for this purpose that the parochial schools had been established, and that encouragement was given to the Scotch Society for the Propagation of Christian Knowledge, which had obtained letters patent from Anne in 1709. This society planted numerous schools all over the Highlands, and made every effort to introduce and maintain the English tongue ; nor was it very long before, even in

the most remote valleys, English was familiar to
the children. When Johnson visited the Highlands he was especially struck by the great effect
of this attack upon the natural language of the
people. Some notion of its virulence may be
obtained from the fact that a movement existed
to prevent the circulation of any Gaelic version
of the Bible; and laws were actually passed
which sought to influence private teachers by
compelling them to take the oath of allegiance.[1]

Although Stone was the first to translate any
of these Gaelic poems, others had previously
been at work collecting them. John Farquharson, a Roman Catholic missionary in Strathglass,
Inverness-shire, and afterwards Prefect of Studies
at Douay,[2] made a large collection some time
before the year 1745. In 1751 Alexander Macdonald, master of the school at Ardnamurchan,
and a well-known Jacobite bard, brought out a
small volume of them at Edinburgh, and in an

[1] After the second Jacobite rising these efforts were re-
doubled, and in 1747 and 1748 culminated in an attempt
to banish the plaid and the kilt. In those years an oath was
administered calling down every kind of misfortune on the
head of the man who should carry gun, sword, or pistol,
or wear a tartan plaid, or any part of the Highland garb.

[2] See *infra*, ch. xiv.

English preface expressed the hope that the
specimens which he offered to the public might
awaken interest in a language which contained
all the charms of poetry and rhetoric, and be-
speak favour for a great collection of such pieces,
illustrating all the kinds of poetry usual among
cultivated nations, with a translation into English verse and critical observations.   Whether
Macdonald's ambitious scheme was examined
and pronounced chimerical, or attracted no attention at all, is a question which cannot now
be determined; but certain it is that it had no
result.   The very existence of Gaelic poetry
continued to be known only to a few persons
outside the Highlands.   But amongst the Highlanders themselves, while it is true that only
here and there any one cared to collect the
specimens which came in his way, a high value
was set upon this rude poetry.   As to the kind
of esteem in which they held it, curious testimony is given by Burt, who visited the north of
Scotland about the year 1730.   He relates that
when he was being entertained at the house of
a Highland chief, the bard attached to the family
repeated an Erse poem for the pleasure of the
guests.   The chief, who prided himself upon his

classical attainments, was loud in his praises of the poem, and declared that some of the passages in it were superior to anything in Virgil or Homer. It is clear, then, that before Macpherson was born there were educated Highlanders who knew and admired this poetry and believed it to be of an epic cast. Of its real nature, so far as our knowledge goes, some account will be given in a subsequent chapter.

Macpherson began to take an interest in it when he was conducting the school at Ruthven. He tells us himself, in the dissertation prefixed to *Fingal,* that he learned to admire Gaelic poetry very early, and gathered some of it from tradition; but that he did so for his own amusement, and without any hope of seeing it in an English dress. He had not far to go to find it. Among the peasantry in Badenoch there were many of the older men who had been little affected by the changes which the zeal of the Government had introduced all over the Highlands since the beginning of the century; in the course of which the institutions of that part of Scotland, its customs, and even, as we have seen, its language, had been in a large measure transformed. Some of these

men had a great mass of Gaelic poetry stored up
in their memory, and they were fond of reciting
to any one who was willing to listen to them.
Macpherson spent some of his spare time in tran-
scribing a few fragments; and we are told by
Ramsay[1] that he did so with no other object
than to amuse himself. The statement is important, and it is perfectly trustworthy. Ramsay
had a wide acquaintance; he was blessed with
the habit of inquiry; he had abundant opportunity of obtaining information from some of his
own contemporaries, who had come into personal
contact with Macpherson; and one[2] at least of
these contemporaries was Macpherson's companion at college, and afterwards his intimate
friend. Ramsay's estimate of Macpherson is in
general so calm, so dispassionate, and so well
supported by other and independent authorities,
that, on the face of it, there is no reason for
doubting the accuracy of any of his particular
assertions.

But the fact, and what it is more important to
establish, the precise nature and extent, of his
interest in Gaelic poetry at this period is proved

[1] *Op. cit.*
[2] Dr. Macleod, of Glasgow.

by evidence much more conclusive than any
one's statement ; namely, the evidence of his own
poetical compositions. As every one knows,
the minor poet at the age of twenty or two-
and-twenty is little but the echo of what
he reads. If Macpherson were influenced by
the beauty of what he had heard recited, we
might expect to find in what he wrote himself
an exact measure of its extent. There is undoubtedly some trace of this influence in *The
Highlander;* but it is slight. It is impossible
for any one to read that poem and not perceive
that the predominating influence there, as in
almost all the poetry of the time, is classical.
Now and then we come upon something in
the imagery which reminds us of the Ossianic
touch ; but it no more lends a tone to the
general effect of the poem than a patch of
wild nature here and there will transform the
character of a trim and ordered garden ; and it
is not because such images are numerous, but
only because they are constantly repeated, that
they make their influence felt at all. The
prevailing character of the poem is the best
evidence obtainable, nay, the best evidence
possible, that Macpherson's original ambition

lay wholly in the line of the general culture
of his day.[1]

There is another circumstance to be borne in
mind in this connection, although it is often
neglected by Macpherson's critics, in spite of its
effect on the larger question of his life.   He had
a very imperfect acquaintance with Gaelic,[2] although the sound of it must have been familiar
to him from his childhood.   At no period of his
career could he have been called a good Gaelic
scholar ; and at this time his education, his
employment, his literary pursuits and ambition
combined to make him neglect a language
that had come to be chiefly spoken by the more
illiterate of the peasantry.

[1] For a purpose of his own, Laing (*op. cit.*) declared that
there was a great resemblance between the Ossianic poems
and Macpherson's early works ; but when he came to prove
his case, he was able to point to only sixteen out of a total
of more than four thousand lines, undoubtedly written by
Macpherson, where any similarity could be traced; and then
it was mostly a similarity of diction, and that, too, of a very
commonplace kind.   Even if any real similarity in these
cases had been fairly made out, the extent of it is not great
enough to prove Laing's contention that Macpherson wrote
the Ossianic poems himself; and conversely, it is not great
enough to prove any large influence of Gaelic poetry on his
early compositions.

[2] On this point see *infra,* pp. 125, 139, 153.

Macpherson continued to teach in the village
school for some time after he left college. This
must have been an irksome task for a poet, a
student of divinity, and a man of culture ; and he
soon sought other employment. Entry into the
ministry was either postponed or altogether
abandoned. He returned to Edinburgh and became a tutor in private families ; although this,
too, according to his own account, was a means
of earning a livelihood not much to his taste.[1]
Towards the end of the year 1758, when he had
reached the age of twenty-two, we find him
settled as tutor in the family of Mr. Graham of
Balgowan, in charge of the young Graham who
afterwards became Lord Lynedoch, and attained
celebrity as one of Wellington's ablest generals.
He devoted his spare time to literature, and, like
most young writers, was glad to do hack-work of
the humblest description. For a part of the
months which he spent in Edinburgh, he was
employed as corrector of the press for Balfour
the publisher.

But although a tutorship was no very agreeable occupation to the proud young Highlander,

[1] Quoted in a letter in Hill Burton's *Life of Hume*, i.
464.

it gave him an opportunity of mixing with men of rank and education ; and it led to incidents which had important results. He accompanied his pupil on a visit to the manse of Logierait, in Perthshire. The minister's son, Adam Ferguson, afterwards well known, had then given up his regimental chaplaincy, and also his position in the Advocates' Library ; and, as far as can be gathered, he was at the manse during young Graham's visit. Macpherson showed him, it is said, some specimens of the Gaelic poetry of the North ; and Ferguson, greatly interested, urged him to enlarge his collection. When he heard that Macpherson was to accompany his pupil in the following summer to Moffat, Ferguson gave him an introduction to a friend there.[1] The acquaintance which ensued made Macpherson's interest in Gaelic poetry no longer a casual amusement, but changed it into a serious business, and opened up a way for him into the best literary society of his time. It will be well to describe the meeting as fully as the evidence allows.

The man whose acquaintance had this impor-

---

[1] The visit to Logierait is given on the authority of a writer in the *Celtic Magazine*, v. 311.

tant effect on Macpherson's subsequent fortunes
was John Home, generally known as "the author
of *Douglas*". Home, though then only thirty-
seven years of age, had already had a varied
career. He fought against the Pretender in
1745 ; he had been captured and imprisoned ;
and, as recorded in *Waverley*, he had escaped by
a rope made of the shreds of his blanket. He
had then taken orders, and in 1746 he became
minister of Athelstaneford in Haddington-
shire. In 1756 his tragedy of *Douglas* was
brought out at Edinburgh ; and in the following
year, through the influence of Lord Bute, at
Covent Garden. It became popular ; but the
fact that a Presbyterian minister had been guilty
of writing a play raised such a storm that Home
was compelled to resign his living. He had,
however, a good friend in Bute, who procured
him the sinecure of Conservator of Scots' Privi-
leges, and later on, a pension, on which he sub-
sisted comfortably to an extreme old age.

In the autumn of 1759 Macpherson went to
Moffat with his pupil and his pupil's mother,
Lady Christian Graham. Lady Christian was a
sister of Lord Hopetoun, who had a house in
the village, and it was there that the party

lodged. Moffat, then as now, was a fashion-
able spa, and Home was drinking the waters.[1]
The general *rendezvous* was the bowling-green;
and there Macpherson made Home's acquaintance. A poor tutor with literary aspirations
was, no doubt, glad to know any one of Home's
reputation; and Home on his part took pleasure
in Macpherson's company; finding him, as he
said, " an exceeding good classical scholar," and
able, moreover, to satisfy an interest which
he had long felt in the subject of Highland
poetry.

Home, who was a Lowlander, has given a
detailed account of this meeting with Macpherson.[2] That the Highlands contained some remains
of ancient Gaelic verse was, he declared, already
known to him by what he had heard from his
friend Adam Ferguson. He was, therefore, very
pleased to meet any one who was a native of the
remote Highlands, and likely to give him some
further information on the same subject. In
reply to his questions Macpherson described

---

[1] Henry Mackenzie's *Works of John Home*, etc., vol. i.,
App., p. 127.

[2] See the *Report of the Highland Society*, App., 68. This
authority will be henceforth quoted as *Rep.*

some of the manners and customs of the Highlanders, and, in particular, how one of their
favourite amusements was to listen to the tales
and compositions of their ancient bards, which
contained much pathos and poetical imagery.
Macpherson added that he remembered several
pieces of this ancient poetry, and had some in
his possession.

Home expressed a desire to see them. Macpherson asked if he understood Gaelic.

"Not one word," said Home.

"Then how can I show you them ?"

"Very easily," replied Home ; "translate one
of the poems which you think a good one, and I
imagine that I shall be able to form some opinion
of the genius and character of the Gaelic poetry."

Macpherson fought shy of the task. It does
not appear that Home was acquainted with the
fact that his young friend had published poetry
of his own ; nor, if he were, is there any record
of his having asked to see it. Moreover, Macpherson was well aware of his own incompetence
as a Gaelic scholar ; and he told Home that any
translation he could make would give a very
imperfect idea of the original. It was only with
great difficulty that Home overcame his scruples.

In a day or two Macpherson reluctantly brought him the fragment of a poem entitled *The Death of Oscar*, and a few days later two or three more fragments.

Macpherson's conduct on this occasion has been turned against him. Those who entirely disbelieved in his alleged discoveries saw in his reluctance nothing but a sign of cowardice, and in the delay of two or three days the most convincing evidence of forgery. And yet these very fragments were afterwards proved to be known in their original to several intelligent and respectable people in different parts of the Highlands.[1] There is no evidence that before this meeting Macpherson had shown any desire to translate such Gaelic poetry as he had collected. Indeed, it is expressly recorded that he had no such desire.[2] It is fair to remember that at the time Macpherson, though ambitious, was very young and completely unknown. To a writer who had become famous he may well have hesitated to exhibit anything of his own; and if he did so, he would hardly wish that it should be only a translation, and an imperfect one. But

[1] See Hume's letter, given on p. 84.
[2] *Rep.*, App., 67.

in order to satisfy Home,—perhaps also to make
the most of this unexpected meeting, he undertook the translation. It was clearly desirable
that he should not execute it hurriedly, and his
employment as tutor did not give him full command of his time.

The first fragment translated by Macpherson
possesses an interest of its own, and some passages of it may be given here. It is quoted in
the form in which it was afterwards published,
which in all probability was not that which was
submitted to Home.

"Why openest thou afresh the spring of my
grief, O son of Alpin, inquiring how Oscar fell?
My eyes are blind with tears; but memory
beams on my heart. How can I relate the
mournful death of the head of the people?
Prince of the warriors, Oscar, my son! shall I
see thee no more?

"He fell as the moon in a storm, as the sun
from the midst of his course, when clouds rise
from the waste of the waves, when the blackness
of the storm inwraps the rocks of Ardanmidder.
I, like an ancient oak on Morven, I moulder
alone in my place. The blast hath lopped my
branches away; and I tremble at the wings of
the north. Prince of the warriors, Oscar, my
son! shall I see thee no more?

"Dermid and Oscar were one; they reaped
the battle together. Their friendship was as
strong as their steel; and death walked between

them to the field. They came on the foe like two rocks falling from the brows of Ardven. Their swords were stained with the blood of the valiant : warriors fainted at their names. . . .

"By the brook of the hill their graves are laid ; a birch's unequal shade covers their tomb. Often on their green earthen tombs the branchy sons of the mountain feed, when midday is all in flames and silence is over all the hills."[1]

Home was extremely pleased at what he regarded as a very important discovery. His account of this meeting is confirmed by a letter[2] from a friend of his, Dr. Alex. Carlyle, of Inveresk, who tells us that on the 2nd of October he came over from the neighbourhood of Dumfries to spend the day with Home at Moffat ; that in the course of conversation Home spoke of his new acquaintance, and the interesting account which he had given of old Gaelic poetry in the Highlands ; and also of the great difficulty in prevailing upon Macpherson to translate some of it which he had by heart.

---

[1] It is said that Macpherson afterwards betrayed the forgery of this poem by applying the elegy to another Oscar, the son of Caruth. But this circumstance does not prove that Macpherson forged the poem : it only proves that he did not know to whom to refer it.

[2] Given in *Rep.*, App., 66.

Carlyle elsewhere [1] records that he was introduced to Macpherson in the bowling-green, and found him to be a big man and good-looking, but proud, reserved, and apparently of an unsociable disposition. He remarked that the young tutor's legs were very thick, and that to hide them he wore boots, which were not then in fashion.

[1] *Autobiography*, p. 398.

CHAPTER IV.

HOME SHOWS THE SPECIMENS TO THE EDINBURGH
"LITERATI".—BLAIR AND MACPHERSON.—
PUBLICATION OF THE "FRAGMENTS".—THEIR
SUCCESS.—OPINIONS OF HUME, GRAY, SHEN-
STONE, MRS. MONTAGU.—MACPHERSON URGED
TO COLLECT MORE.—HIS RELUCTANCE.

HOME took the translations with him to Edinburgh, and there showed them to his friends.
At no other time was there gathered together
in the Scottish capital so large and so distinguished a company of men of letters ; and
although its lustre is now somewhat dim, it was
a very famous company in its day. Whether in
philosophical and sociological speculation, or in
historical learning, or in the mere bulk and
literary skill of their productions, the Scottish
men of letters were at the moment far in ad-
vance of their English contemporaries. As we
look back upon them, David Hume towers
above the rest ; but Kaimes and Monboddo,
Lords of Session, were also acute philosophers ;
and their disquisitions on the origins of man

(72)

and of language and the moral sentiments in some ways anticipated modern theories. In this "Select Circle," as it was called, were also to be found Robertson the historian, Lord Elibank, and Home himself; and of the outlying members the most important was Adam Smith, then a professor at Glasgow. These were men perfectly competent to form an opinion on any matter of literary interest; and at the time no severer test could be devised for Macpherson's work than to ask their judgment upon it.

The dominant member of the circle was Dr. Hugh Blair, literary critic and theologian, now remembered—or perhaps hardly remembered— as the prolific author of rhetorical sermons. By dint of hard work and good fortune he had made a great reputation, and was then beginning to be regarded as the literary dictator of the north. To him the translations were submitted, with a result highly satisfactory to Macpherson, who found himself transformed from a poor and obscure tutor into a person of great interest to the most conspicuous writers of his country. Blair did so much to help Macpherson at the time, and was afterwards so intimately connected with the success of his work, that it

will be well to let him tell his own tale of
the part which he played in giving these first
translations to the world.

"Being," he wrote, "as much struck as Mr.
Home with the high spirit of poetry which
breathed in them, I presently made inquiry
where Mr. Macpherson was to be found ; and
having sent for him to come to me, had much
conversation with him on the subject.   When I
learned that, besides the few pieces of that
poetry which he had in his possession, greater
and more considerable poems of the same strain
were to be found in the Highlands, and were
well known to the natives there, I urged him to
translate the other pieces which he had, and
bring them to me ; promising that I should take
care to circulate and bring them out to the
public, by whom they were well deserved to be
known.   He was extremely reluctant and averse
to complying with my request, saying that no
translation of his could do justice to the spirit
and force of the original ; and that besides in-
juring them by translation, he apprehended that
they would be very ill relished by the public, as
so very different from the strain of modern ideas,
and of modern, connected, and polished poetry.[1]
It was not until after much and repeated impor-
tunity on my part and representing to him the
injustice he would do to his native country by
keeping concealed those hidden treasures, which,
I assured him, if brought forth, would serve to
enrich the whole learned world, that I at length

[1] Macpherson himself re-states this objection in the dissertation prefixed to *Fingal*.

prevailed on him to translate, and to bring to me, the several poetic pieces which he had in his possession." [1]

Macpherson's reluctance to comply with so flattering a request has nearly always been explained on the supposition that he was a forger anxious for his own safety. Few or none of his adverse critics knew anything of his life previous to the incident at Moffat. Doubting his honesty, they had to explain his conduct; and they proceeded to declare that his reluctance was at first the outcome of mere affectation, and then an expression of genuine alarm lest he should be unable to carry out the imposture he was planning, in the face of such distinguished critics as Blair and his friends.

This seems to be an explanation more difficult to understand than the fact which it proposes to explain. Up to the moment Macpherson had received nothing but encouragement, unmingled with any breath of suspicion; and if he had been a mere forger he would have already won complete confidence in himself by his easy conquest of the best of his

[1] *Rep.*, App., 57.

contemporaries. Some indication of what was probably the real reason has already been given; and it is confirmed by the statement of one of his intimate friends at this time, a Mr. George Laurie, who, about twenty years later, declared that he had several letters from Macpherson in which he begged to be released from his promise, chiefly on the ground, as he expressed it, "that his Highland pride was alarmed at appearing to the world only as a translator".[1] These words have been twisted out of their natural sense, and held to imply that Macpherson wished in reality to be acknowledged as the author rather than as the translator of the fragments, but that he had already gone so far on the path of imposture that he was unable now to turn back. But if the words are taken in an obvious and unprejudiced sense, they afford an explanation of Macpherson's conduct much more probable in itself, and more consonant with all that we know of his position at the time. Annoyed at the neglect which had attended his own efforts as an original poet, he was in no mind to be satisfied with the inferior *rôle* of translating the poems of others, however successfully; and

[1] Laing, *op. cit.*, i. xv.

of his success even in this humbler sphere he was, as has been seen, by no means confident. No one who had seen his original work fall unnoticed from the press, would be likely to welcome a proposal that he should make a second appearance only as the translator of matter the very existence of which was almost unknown to the literary world. In all probability Macpherson was fairly astonished at the interest aroused by the poems ; and undoubtedly he never imagined that the work to which he was urged to put his hand would have the enormous success which awaited it, and within a few years profoundly influence the literature of Europe. It would be too much to expect of human nature that he should think less of his own lengthy works than of the few fragments of rude verse which he had picked up in the wilds of his native district.

But Blair was too great a potentate to be resisted. Macpherson saw his fragments handed about amongst people of taste, and everywhere admired. In January, 1760, Sir David Dalrymple sent them to Horace Walpole at Strawberry Hill; and in writing to acknowledge them Walpole expressed a high opinion of their beauty, and the natural character of their images and their sentiment.[1] Through the carelessness of transcribers, the poems were corrupted, so that in the end Macpherson was compelled to print them in self-defence.[2] He at first, it is said,[3] intended to send them to a magazine, but some judicious friend advised a more imposing method of giving them to the world. Encouraged by Blair, who probably strengthened him in the idea that the fragments were parts of a larger work, Macpherson, still employed in Mr. Graham's family, completed the translation of some sixteen pieces. In June, 1760, these were published at Edinburgh in a small thin volume, under the title *Fragments of Ancient Poetry collected in the Highlands of Scotland and translated from the Galic or Erse Language.* Blair superintended their production ; and, as the result of various conversations with Macpherson, himself wrote the preface.

He explained to the public that the work contained genuine remains of Scottish poetry,

[1] *Walpole's Letters*, ed. Cunningham, iii. 184, dated 3rd Feb., 1760.

[2] Preface to *Fingal*.

[3] *Encyclopædia Britannica*, 3rd edit. (Edin., 1801), Supplement, i. 108.

—of uncertain date, indeed, but still, if tradition were true, of great antiquity, and betraying their age by the ideas and the manners which they represented. They must, he urged, be anterior to the establishment of the clan system, itself very ancient; for they contained no mention of it, nor any trace of the influence of Christianity, or, indeed, of any religion. He proceeded to describe them as probably episodes of a greater work, narrating the wars of a hero of whom there were innumerable traditions; and he had no doubt that the poems were to be ascribed to the bards, a race of men well known to have continued throughout many ages in Ireland and the north of Scotland. He believed that many more such remains of ancient genius might be found in the Highlands; in particular, a heroic poem, of considerable length, treating of the invasion of Ireland by the Danes, the preparations made to resist it by Cuchulaid, the Irish leader, the councils that were held, and the battles that were fought, until at last the Irish were compelled to submit; how, then, Fingal, King of Scotland, came to their help with his ships, expelled the Danes, and returned victorious. This poem was held to be of greater

antiquity than the others, and the author spoke
of himself as present in the expedition.

Although a specimen of these *Fragments*
has already been given, it will be convenient to
quote a few further passages here.

"Evening is grey on the hills. The north
wind resounds through the woods. White
clouds rise on the sky; the trembling snow
descends. The river howls afar, along its wind-
ing course. Sad, by a hollow rock, the grey-haired
Carryl sat. Dry fern waves over his head; his
seat is an aged birch. Clear to the roaring
winds he lifts his voice of woe.

"Tossed on the wavy ocean is he, the hope of
the isles; Malcolm, the support of the poor; foe
to the proud in arms; why hast thou left us
behind? why have we to mourn thy fate?"

"Son of the noble Fingal, Ossian, prince of
men! what tears run down the cheeks of age?
what shakes thy mighty soul?

"Memory, son of Alpin, memory wounds the
aged. Of former times are my thoughts; my
thoughts are of the noble Fingal. The race of
the king returns into my mind, and wounds me
with remembrance. . . .

"Son of Alpin! the woes of the aged are many;
their tears are for the past. This raised my
sorrow, warrior; memory awaked my grief.
Oscar, my son, was brave; but Oscar is now no
more. Thou hast heard my grief, O son of
Alpin! forgive the tears of the aged."

"By the side of a rock on the hill, beneath
the aged tree, old Ossian sat on the moss; the

last of the race of Fingal. Sightless are his aged eyes; his beard is waving in the wind. Dull through the leafless trees he heard the voice of the north. Sorrow revived in his soul; he began and lamented the dead."

The translation of these poems into measured prose, instead of into the traditional channel of poetical expression at the time, the ten-syllable couplet, was a very wise proceeding; it was continued and perfected in the later poems; and it had more to do with the success of Macpherson's work than is commonly perceived or acknowledged. It was not with him that the idea originated. He tells us [1] that he at first intended to publish in verse, as he thought that the prose version, however novel or harmonious, would not, to the ordinary reader, make up for the absence of the frequent returns of rhyme; but he yielded to the judgment of others, "in a mode which presented freedom and dignity of expression, instead of fetters to cramp the thought". It was, he said, a gentleman who had made himself a figure in the poetical world, that gave him the first hints concerning a literal prose translation; he tried it at his desire,

[1] Preface to the fourth edition of *Fingal*, and the dissertation prefixed to the first edition.

and the specimen was approved. Ramsay tells
us that this gentleman was generally supposed
to be Home.[1] On the other hand, Laing[2] declared that Macpherson took the idea from
Louth's explanation of the nature of Hebrew
poetry, which Blair had introduced into his
lectures. The likeness between Macpherson's
measured prose and the style of the psalms
and prophetical works of the Old Testament
is sufficiently obvious.

The success of the little volume was instan-
taneous and complete. A second edition appeared almost immediately, with some slight
alterations, drawn, as the translator noted, from
more complete copies which he had obtained of
the originals. The *Fragments* soon made their
way into England, where they were reprinted in
some of the magazines of the time. Three of them,
for instance, appeared in the *Annual Register* for
the year 1760; with the remark that there was
far less doubt of their merit than of their authenticity. It is a curious fact that an attempt was
at once made to turn some of the fragments into
verse, for in the same publication two of them

[1] See Ramsay, *loc. cit.*
[2] *Op. cit.*, ii. 436.

appeared in rhymed heroics. One of these versifications hailed from Birmingham in the same month in which the original had been published in Edinburgh. Some attempt was made to imitate them, and there were one or two parodies.

The discussion of the age of the *Fragments* led naturally to the question of their authenticity; and from the beginning, as might have been expected with a production of the kind, it was seriously debated. One of the first to take the matter up was Hume, who was then in Edinburgh. In his letters on the subject, and in an essay on the authenticity of the later poems,[1] he has left on record his judgment on the whole matter, expressed with his luminous grace; and as his letters give an interesting picture of Macpherson, and the effect which he produced upon the philosopher, no excuse is needed for drawing largely upon them here.

The following passages are from a letter to an unknown correspondent, ostensibly written to draw an opinion from Gray.

[1] Both the essay and the letters are given in Hill Burton's *Life of Hume*, vol. i., App., 462.

"Edinburgh, 16th August, 1760.

" I am not surprised to find by your letter that Mr. Gray should have entertained suspicions with regard to the authenticity of these fragments of our Highland poetry. The first time I was shown the copies of some of them in manuscript by our friend John Home, I was inclined to be a little incredulous on that head ; but Mr. Home removed my scruples by informing me of the manner in which he procured them from Mr. Macpherson, the translator. . . .

" After this volume was in everybody's hands, and universally admired, we heard every day new reasons which put the authenticity, not the great antiquity which the translator ascribes to them, beyond all question ; for their antiquity is a point which must be ascertained by reasoning ; though the arguments he employs seem very probable and convincing. But certain it is that these poems are in everybody's mouth in the Highlands, have been handed down from father to son, and are of an age beyond all memory and tradition.

" In the family of every Highland chieftain there was anciently retained a bard whose office was the same with that of the Greek rhapsodists, and the general subject of the poems which he recited was the wars of Fingal, an epoch no less remarkable among them than the wars of Troy among the Greek poets. This custom is not even yet altogether abolished : the bard and the piper are esteemed the most honourable offices in a chieftain's family, and these two characters are frequently united in the same person. Adam Smith, the celebrated professor in Glasgow, told me that the piper of the Argyleshire Militia

repeated to him all those poems which Mr. Macpherson has translated, and many more of equal
beauty. Major Mackay, Lord Reay's brother,
also told me that he remembers them perfectly,
as also did the Laird of Macfarlane, the greatest
antiquarian whom we have in the country, and
who insists so strongly on the historical truth,
as well as on the poetical beauty of these productions. I could add the Laird and Lady
Macleod to these authorities, with many more,
if these were not sufficient, as they live in different parts of the Highlands, very remote from
each other, and they could only be acquainted
with poems that had become in a manner
national works, and had gradually spread themselves into every mouth, and imprinted themselves on every memory."

Hume later on returned to the incredulity
with which he had at first received Macpherson's productions. But it is curious to find him
here adducing unimpeachable testimony to the
genuineness of the *Fragments*, and employing the
very method which, as he afterwards insisted,
was alone adequate to determine their authenticity. He declared, with obvious justice, that
the truth of the matter could only be established
by an accumulation of particular testimonies ;
but when he himself came to judge of Macpherson's productions as a whole, he proceeded on
grounds almost purely critical and *a priori*, of

which the following extract from the same letter
may serve as an example.

" I own that my first and chief objection to the
authenticity of these fragments was not on account of the noble and even tender strokes which
they contain ; for these are the offspring of genius
and passion in all countries ; I was only surprised at the regular plan which appears in some
of these pieces, and which seems to be the work
of a more cultivated age.   None of the specimens
of barbarous poetry known to us, the Hebrew,
Arabian, or any other, contains this species of
beauty ; and if a regular epic poem, or even anything of that kind, nearly regular, should also
come from that rough climate and uncivilised
people, it would appear to me a phenomenon
altogether unaccountable."

But, on the whole, he found most reason to
believe the *Fragments* genuine.

" I forgot," he said, " to mention, ·as another
proof of the authenticity of these poems, and
even of the reality of the adventures contained
in them, that the names of the heroes, Fingal,
Oscar, Osur, Oscan, Dermid, are still given in
the Highlands to large mastiffs, in the same
manner as we affix to them the names of Cæsar,
Pompey, Hector, or the French that of Marlborough.
    " It gives me pleasure to find that a person
of so fine a taste as Mr. Gray approves of these
fragments ; as it may convince us that our fond-
ness of them is not altogether founded on

national prepossessions, which, however, you
know to be a little strong. The translation is
elegant."

Gray had, indeed, formed a high opinion of
the *Fragments*. Some of them had been sent
to him in manuscript, and he had corresponded
with Macpherson. At the beginning he expressed some doubt.

" I wrote to Scotland," he told Wharton,[1] " to
make a thousand inquiries ; the letters I have in
return are ill-wrote, ill-reasoned, unsatisfactory,
calculated (one would imagine) to deceive, and
yet not cunning enough to do it cleverly. In
short, the whole external evidence would make
me believe these fragments counterfeit ; but the
internal is so strong on the other side, that I am
resolved to believe them genuine, spite of the
Devil and the Kirk ; it is impossible to conceive
that they were written by the same man that
writes me these letters ; on the other hand it is
almost as hard to suppose (if they are original)
that he should be able to translate them so
admirably. In short, the man is the very demon
of poetry, or he has lighted on a treasure hid for
ages."

The general opinion at Cambridge, according
to Gray's statement, was that the poems were
spurious ; but he himself, although puzzled, con-

[1] Mason's *Life of Gray* (edit. 1807), ii. 162.

tinued to believe them old : "whether they are
inventions of antiquity or of a modern Scotchman, either case is to me alike unaccountable ".[1]

He was especially struck by "the nature and
noble wild imagination" of *The Song of the Six
Bards*, a curious fragment which Macpherson
sent to him in manuscript; and he wrote to a
friend to praise it.

"The oddest thing is that every one of them
(the five bards and the chieftain) sees ghosts,
more or less.   The idea that struck and surprised me most is the following.   One of them,
describing a storm of wind and rain, says :—

'Ghosts ride on the tempest to-night.
Sweet is their voice between the gusts of wind.
Their songs are of other worlds.'

Did you never observe (*while rocking winds are
piping loud*) that pause, as the gust is recol-
lecting itself, and rising upon the ear in a *shrill*
and plaintive note, like the swell of an Æolian
harp?   I do assure you there is nothing in the
world so like the voice of a spirit."

That Macpherson should have been unable
to return a satisfactory answer to Gray's "thousand inquiries" is hardly surprising.   Of their
exact nature nothing can now be ascertained ;
but they were probably directed to the historical

[1] Mason's *Life of Gray*, pp. 167, 173.

and antiquarian aspect of the poems. Of this Macpherson could give only the vague traditional account ; embellished, it may be, by crude speculations of his own ; and these speculations, if we may judge by their development in the preface to *Fingal*, were not of a character to recommend themselves to a man of Gray's profound and accurate learning. Nor, indeed, was Gray much influenced by them in forming his opinion.

Specimens of the *Fragments* were also sent to Shenstone, who took a lively interest in them, and in the further proposal for the publication of the epic poem. It is a curious fact that long before Macpherson produced his *Fingal*, its size and character should have been discussed by the literary gossips of the time. One of Shenstone's correspondents, writing in June, 1760, gives us some of this gossip ; and records, among other things, that the epic was generally said to consist of upwards of 9000 lines.[1]

From Gray and Shenstone the *Fragments* and *The Song of the Six Bards* found their way to Lord Lyttelton, who refused to believe in their authenticity. He sent them to Mrs. Montagu,

[1] Hull's *Select Letters* (London, 1778), ii. 167.

and they won the favour of that well-known
lady.   In an interesting letter written in October, 1760, she gave some expression to the
prevailing doubt as to their authenticity; but
she declared that on the whole she found it
impossible to disbelieve that they were old; in
spite, as she added, of what Lord Marchmount
told her, that the old Highland bard was a
modern gentleman of his acquaintance.[1]

The wide interest roused by the *Fragments*
immediately led to a general desire in Edinburgh
that any other remains of Gaelic poetry which
might still exist in the Highlands should be
recovered and collected.   On the 23rd of June,
a week or two after the publication of the *Fragments,* Blair wrote to Lord Hailes on the subject,
and expressed a desire that some scheme might
be discovered " for encouraging **Mr.** Macpherson
to apply himself to the making a further collection of Earse poetry, and particularly for recovering *our epic,*"[2] and proposed a subscription
to defray the expense of a search.   The work
of anglicising the Highlands was proceeding so

[1] Mrs. Montagu's *Letters* (edition of 1813), iv. 317. This
Lord Marchmount was the friend and executor of Pope.
    [2] Laing, *op. cit.*, i. xvi.

fast that unless a search for these remains were made at once, there was little chance of recovering any considerable number of them. Macpherson, it was agreed, was in all respects the right man to make it, and he was strongly urged to do so.

But here, again, he expressed extreme reluctance. He was asked to spend a great deal of time and energy in prosecuting, in a thorough and systematic fashion, a species of literary work of which, when it was first proposed to him in a very small way, he had clearly shown that he was by no means enamoured. He now urged that he was diffident of success; and certainly, to speak vaguely of poems scattered about the Highlands, and to allow Blair to proclaim their existence to the public as fragments of a great epic, was one thing; and to go and find them, another. He repeated his fears that such poems, even if discovered, would be ill suited to the general taste. Finally, he explained the difficulty of such a search as was necessary in wild and remote districts, and the expense which it would involve.

Macpherson, as Blair tells us, was not a man very ready to take advice; and for some two

months he hesitated. However ready he may
have been to give up his position as a tutor, his
prospect of obtaining a definite livelihood would
undoubtedly suffer by doing so. His whole attitude at the time, when it is remembered that
he was barely twenty-four, was not of a kind to
lend itself to suspicion. Hume was taken with
him, though he afterwards had occasion to alter
his opinion. "We have endeavoured," he wrote,

"to put Mr. Macpherson on a way of procuring
us more of these wild flowers. He is a modest,
sensible, young man, not settled in any living,
but employed as a private tutor in Mr. Graham
of Balgowan's family, a way of life which he is
not fond of. We have, therefore, set about a
subscription of a guinea or two guineas apiece,
in order to enable him to quit that family, and
undertake a mission into the Highlands, where
he hopes to recover more of these fragments."

To stimulate interest in the undertaking,
Blair arranged that some of the leaders of rank
and taste in Edinburgh should meet at a dinner
to which Macpherson was invited. Lord Elibank
played a great part at it, together with Robertson, Home, Adam Ferguson, and many others,
who were all very anxious to forward the scheme.
After much conversation with Macpherson, it

was agreed that he should disengage himself
from all other employment, and set out without
delay on a poetical mission throughout the
Highlands ; and as his circumstances did not
admit of his engaging in this at his own expense,
the whole cost of his journey was to be defrayed
by a collection raised from those present at the
meeting, and any other friends who might be
disposed to assist them.   Robert Chalmers
undertook to collect the money, and to act
as treasurer.   " I remember well," said Blair,[1]

" that when the company was about to break up,
and I was going away, Mr. Macpherson followed
me to the door, and told me that from the spirit
of that meeting he now for the first time entertained the hope that the undertaking to which I
had so often prompted him would be attended
with success ; that hitherto he had imagined they
were merely romantic ideas which I had held

[1] *High. Soc. Rep.*, App., 58.   In the face of so much testimony to the contrary, it is impossible to prove, what has
been often idly asserted, that Macpherson's reluctance was
not genuine.   Further, there is no evidence to show that it
was he who urged that the *Fragments* in question were parts
of an epic poem.   Blair's strenuous insistence on this point in
his *Critical Dissertation* points to the probability that he, and
not Macpherson, broached the idea.   Macpherson's allusion
to the " romantic ideas " which Blair held out to him, is
important in this connection, and has not, I think, attracted

out to him; but he now saw them likely to be
realised, and should endeavour to acquit himself
so as to give satisfaction to all his friends."

Money was freely promised at the dinner;
and a subscription list, opened in the Parliament
House, brought in £60. Macpherson gave up
his tutorship, and prepared to undertake the
search. We learn from Mrs. Montagu that he
received £100 to defray the expenses of his
journey.[1]

sufficient attention. It is true that in the first note to
Temora, bk. i., he says that the title of epic was imposed on
that poem by himself. But that was in 1763, subsequent
to Blair's *Dissertation*, which Macpherson then accepted as
the most authoritative criticism.

[1] *Letters, ibid.*

CHAPTER V.

THE ENTHUSIASM IN EDINBURGH.—ANCIENT GAELIC
POETRY.—THE IRISH AND THE SCOTCH TRA-
DITION.—" THE DEAN OF LISMORE'S BOOK."
—CARSEWELL'S " BOOK OF COMMON ORDER".
—SCOTCH MANUSCRIPTS.—ORAL RECITATION
AND THE BARDS.—CONDITION OF SCOTCH-
GAELIC POETRY IN MACPHERSON'S TIME.—
HIS CRITICAL EFFORTS.—HIS ATTITUDE TO
IRISH-GAELIC POETRY.

THE popular fashion in literature at the end of
the nineteenth century has little in common with
the fashion which reigned in the middle of the
eighteenth; and the reader who delights in the
kind of books at present in vogue, will be at
a loss to understand how any popular interest
could have been excited in Edinburgh in the
year 1760 by an elegant version of a few old
Gaelic poems. Nor will the commotion which
the translator produced be any the more intelligible to the severe student imbued with modern
methods of antiquarian research. Yet the enthusiasm which touched our great-grandfathers
at the mere prospect of discovering a lost epic

in the remote valleys of the north was perfectly genuine ; and so far was it from being confined to a third- or fourth-rate literary clique, that it was the first writers of the time who were most completely carried away by it. Men so different in mental qualities, in literary aims, tastes, and capacities, as Blair, Hume, and Gray, while they varied in their opinion of the merits of this poetry, shared the common astonishment to the full, and, as appears by the evidence, were more eager than Macpherson himself to collect as much of it as could be found. It will help us to realise their enthusiasm if we remember that they formed their opinion solely on the translator's version. The criticism of the day was a criticism of taste and sentiment ; with a few notable exceptions, it was the elegance and refinement of so-called polite learning‘ rather than any scientific precision, that made the strongest appeal. Of the real nature, origin, and history of the poems, the critics knew nothing ; and in order to arrive at a fair understanding of Macpherson's work, and of the way in which he dealt with his materials, a slight knowledge of these matters will be necessary.

That some rude poetry existed in many parts
of the Highlands is a fact which every one ad-
mits now, and even in the last century none
but the more violent and ignorant of the con-
troversialists disputed it. Macpherson's success,
by whatever means he attained it, incited others
to the work of collection ; but most of those
who followed him were inspired by antiquarian
rather than by literary ambition. Of these the
latest and most important was J. F. Campbell
of Islay, whose *Leabhar na Feinne* contains a
quantity of Highland poetry indisputably genuine, collected partly from oral tradition and
partly from manuscripts of various date, some
of them as old as 1512. Campbell's collection
consists of ballads and short poems in the rough
condition in which they were actually found ;
and it is there that the exact nature of the
Gaelic poetry of the Highlands can best be
studied, and the most accurate account be obtained of the legends which they embodied. But
the general character of the legends was well
known in Macpherson's day ; and even then it
was abundantly proved that a rude poetry, re-
counting the doings of a great chief or hero,
named Fion or Fingal, had been handed down

among the Highlanders from time immemorial.
Common sayings, popular proverbs, and local
names in the Highlands and Isles everywhere
attested this belief; so that the poems and
ballads, and the heroism which they celebrated,
were regarded as the ancient heritage of the
Caledonians.

But when we go further and inquire into
the origin of this poetry, we come to matters
that are in high dispute. That its substance
is not very modern is almost the only thing
about it upon which every one will agree.
The tradition of Fingal and the Feinne dates
from a time when there was little or no racial
distinction between the inhabitants of the
Highlands and Western Isles and those of the
North of Ireland; and as it belonged to both
in the past, it has become a bone of contention between them in the present. We know
on the unquestioned authority of the *Book of
Leinster*, compiled in the earlier half of the
twelfth century, and one of the most valuable
and ancient Irish manuscripts extant, that
Finn MacCumhaill was a personage of much
renown in early Irish tradition; his pedigree
is there given at great length; and in the *Annals*

of the Four Masters [1] it is recorded that he was slain in battle A.D. 283 in the reign of Cairbre Lifeachair. We have an account, also in the *Book of Leinster*, of a great slaughter at Gabhra in the following year, when the Feinne were overthrown, and Oscar, son of Ossian, son of Finn MacCumhaill, was killed. It is certain that the memory of these deeds was celebrated in song and preserved by tradition; for the same book gives the incidents of the battle as they were described in an ancient poem attributed to Ossian or Oisin. Now, whoever Finn MacCumhaill was, in tradition he appears to be the same person as Fingal. On these and other grounds the Irish claim Fingal and Ossian for their own.

But the Scotch also claim them. In this same poem in the *Book of Leinster* Feinne from all quarters are mentioned : not only Feinne of Erin, but Feinne of Alban or Scotland, of Breatan, the district of Dumbarton, and of Lochlan, the name given to the North of

---

[1] The chief of them was Michael O'Clery, a Franciscan friar, who, in 1632, compiled the *Annals* from then existing Irish manuscripts. They extend from a fabulous antiquity to the year 1616.

Germany between the Rhine and the Elbe, and
later to Denmark and Norway; and as it seems
clear that Cairbre was King of Ireland at the
time, it seems also clear that some at any rate of
the Feinne were invaders. The Scotch declare
that Fingal was King of Morven. Certain it is
that names recalling the Feinne are still to be
found in various parts of the Highlands, in
Athole, Lochaber, Glenelg, and elsewhere;
and that these names are ancient is proved by
ancient documents. The names of Cuchullin,
too, and the sons of Uisneach, who play a large
part in Irish tradition of a still earlier date, are
also well known in the Western Isles, where we
have the Cuchullin Hills, Glen Uisneach and the
vitrified forts known as Dun Mhic Uisneachan.

Of the Feinne all that we know is that they
were heroic warriors fighting against extinction.
The burden of all their ballads is that they went
forth to the battle, but that they always fell.
But to ask who Fingal really was, whether he
flourished in Ireland or in Scotland, or whether
he was not an entirely mythical personage,
akin to, if not identical with, King Arthur;
whether his faithless spouse Graine is not
the faithless Guinevere with a new name;

to ask who the Feinne were, whence they
came, what they did, how they stood to
other tribes of whom we have mention, the
Cruithne and the Tuatha dé Danann, and in
what direction they disappeared; where, when,
and by whom their deeds were first sung, and
how these songs were preserved,—is to ask
questions to which, in spite of much writing, no
certain answer has yet been given.[1]

In connection with Macpherson's search it
will be desirable to show that the tales of
Fingal and his heroes, of Cuchullin, Derdriu,
and the sons of Uisneach, were the subject of

---

[1] If the reader desires to take an accurate survey of the
present state of these questions, let me recommend him to
peruse the thirty volumes of the following works: *Transactions of the Dublin Ossianic Society*, 1854-61, six vols.;
O'Curry's *Manners and Customs of the Ancient Irish*, three
vols.; Hardiman's *Irish Minstrelsy;* Drummond's *Ancient
Irish Minstrelsy;* M. d'Arbois de Jubainville's *Cours de
Litterature Celtique*, i., ii., and v.; Skene's *Celtic Scotland*,
three vols., his Introd. to *The Dean of Lismore's Book*,
and his *Essay on the Highlanders;* Hill Burton's *History of
Scotland*, i., ii.; Reeves' edition of Adamnan's *Life of St.
Columba;* J. F. Campbell's *Leabhar na Feinne*, and *Tales of
the West Highlands*, four vols., and his review of Clerk's
Ossian in the *Times*, 15th April, 1871; Macneill's *Literature
of the Highlanders;* *La Revue Celtique*, *passim;* Ebrard's
Finghal, etc.

popular song in Scotland from a very early date.
For this purpose it is unnecessary to distinguish
between the three cycles or classes which
scholars have established in Irish mythology
and heroic tradition. In the earliest life of St.
Columba, the first and greatest of the Irish
missionaries to Scotland, written in the seventh
century, three places are mentioned in connection with his journey to the palace of the King
of the Picts; namely, Cainle, Arcardan, and the
river Nesae. The names of the three sons of
Uisneach were Ainle, Ardan, and Naoise;[1] and
two vitrified forts near Lochness are called
Dundeardhuil. It is also said that mention is
made of Fingal in one of the early lives of St.
Columba. Giraldus Cambrensis (d. 1220) referred
to a Gaelic poet named Ossian. On the other
hand, there are some who assert that the
Ossianic legend, describing the invasion of the
Lochlanners, is not older than the eleventh
and twelfth centuries, and that it was formed
by mingling stories of the Northmen's invasion
in the ninth century with early heroic traditions.
The oldest version of the tale of Derdriu is
found in the Glenmasan manuscripts, dated 1238,

[1] See Skene's Introd. to *The Dean's Book*, lxxxi.

now in the Advocates' Library at Edinburgh. In John Barbour's poem of *The Bruce*, written about the year 1375, there is a verse on Fingal, and on Gaul, the son of Morn :—

> " He said methink Marchokys son
> Right as Gol Mak Morn was won,
> To haiff fra Fyngal his menye
> Rycht sua all his fra us has he ".
> —(Book iii.)

The humanist Arthur Johnston in the same century spoke of great epic poems of the Gaels. Hector Boethius in his *History of Scotland* printed at Paris in 1526, in mentioning Arthur and other ancient British worthies in history and legend, also spoke of Fingal as a remarkable figure in early Scottish tradition : " Conjiciunt quidam in hæc tempora Fynnanum filium cœli (Fyn Mak Coul vulgari vocabulo) virum, uti ferunt, immani statura, Scotici sanguinis," etc. Gavin Douglas, on the other hand, in his *Palice of Honour* (before 1522), described Fingal as a deified hero of Ireland :—

> " Greit Gow Macmorne, and Fyn Mac Cowl, and how
> They suld be goddis in Ireland as they say ".

But this, again, is contradicted by a passage in *The Interlude of the Droichis :—*

" My fore grandsyr, hecht Fyn Mac Cowl,
  That dang the devil and gart him yowll,
  The skyis rained when he wald scowll
  And trublit all the air.

" He gat my grandschir Gog Magog,
  Ay when he dansit the warld wald schog
  Five thousand ellis yeid in his frog
  Of hieland pladdis of hair."

Still more valuable evidence of the widespread
existence of this poetry is at hand in *The Dean
of Lismore's Book.* This is a manuscript of the
early part of the sixteenth century, containing
over eleven thousand verses of Gaelic poetry
ascribed to various bards, and among them
twenty-eight poems of an Ossianic character,
nine of them ascribed to Ossian himself, and
the rest to immediate contemporaries or suc-
cessors. It belonged to M'Gregor, Dean of Lismore, which was then the Metropolitan Church
of the See of Argyle. The dates affixed to it
show that it was written at various periods between the years 1512 and 1529. If *The Dean's
Book* establishes nothing else, it is conclusive
evidence that the names and events which afterwards formed the staple of Macpherson's translations were the subject of popular poetry in the
sixteenth century. Later on in that century the

Book of the Common Order of the Kirk of Scotland by John Knox, printed in English in 1565, was, in 1567, translated into Gaelic by Carsewell, Bishop of Argyle and the Isles. It was the first book printed in that language ; and in his preface the bishop deplored the fact that the Highlanders much preferred their ancient ballads — " vain, tempting, lying, worldly histories, concerning the Tuatha dé Danann and warriors and champions, and Fingal the son of Cumhall with his heroes "—to such godly works as he was about to publish. And Kirk, in his translation of the *Psalms of David* into Gaelic as late as the year 1684, sends it out into the world with these lines : —

"Little volume, go boldly forth,
   Raise whom ye reach to pure and Godly strains,
   Hail the generous land of Fingal's heroes
   The Highland tracts and Isles of Hebrides ".

Even those who, in face of many difficulties, contend for the Highland origin of Fingal and Ossian, are ready to allow that the poems and ballads relating their great deeds on Irish soil are likely to have been known and sung by the Irish bards who in early centuries came over in large numbers to Scotland, in the train, perhaps,

of the Irish missionaries. It is, however, no
part of the business of the present volume to
offer an opinion on this international dispute.
For many centuries after St. Columba's time
there was a free interchange of Gaelic learning,
just as there was a political union, between
the two countries. There is the important
fact to be remembered, that, of Gaelic
manuscripts extant, by far the larger number
come from Ireland ; and if any large number
ever existed in Scotland at any period of its
history, the fact has yet to be proved. It is
asserted on behalf of the Scottish contention,
that civil and religious troubles in the Highlands were more inimical to the preservation
of manuscripts than similar troubles in Ireland.
The Scotch point to the monastery of Iona
or Icolmkill, which, if tradition be trustworthy,
was an Irish missionary establishment, as the
head and centre of Gaelic learning in Scotland.
There is, it is true, some slight tradition to
show that manuscripts were once collected
there. Hector Boethius records that about
the year 800, Eugene VII. ordered all books
and manuscripts relating to the history of Scotland to be deposited at Iona in a new build-

ing specially erected for the purpose; and that some of the manuscripts there had been taken in the sacking of Rome by Fergus II. when he assisted Alaric the Goth in the year 410. But if there were any manuscripts at Iona at the end of the eighth century, they would hardly have escaped destruction in the hands of the Scandinavian pirates in the ninth. If a further collection was made in the next four centuries, that, too, say the Scotch, was destroyed in the year 1296, by Edward I.[1] And if anything survived these two attacks, it was carried off to Douay and to Rome at the time of the Reformation. If there was anything at Douay it disappeared in the French Revolution, for the monastery was burned to the ground in 1793. This summary fashion of accounting for the paucity of Gaelic manuscripts in Scotland reduces us to look for them amongst the as yet undiscovered treasures of the Vatican.[2]

[1] Hume says that "Edward I. gave orders to destroy the records and all the monuments of antiquity which might preserve the memory of the independence of the kingdom, and refute the English claims of superiority". It might be difficult to obtain any precise evidence for this statement.

[2] We have some strange evidence of the destruction of private collections. Father Farquharson (see *infra,* ch. xiv.)

108

JAMES MACPHERSON.

It was almost entirely in the Highlands that
the poems and ballads which existed in Scotland,
probably from early times, but to our certain
knowledge as early as the twelfth century, were
handed down. The state of that region up
to the early part of the eighteenth century, the
ignorance of every civilised art, the barbarous
character of almost every pursuit, and the effort
made by the Church, the sole literary influence,
to discourage the recitation of all such poems,
combined to restrict their spread. The few individuals who devoted themselves to literature
took no notice of them; although, as is evident
from *The Dean's Book,* some attempt must
have been made from time to time to collect
them. And it is a curious and noteworthy fact
that one of the pieces there collected refers to
the practice of writing down such poetry.[1] But
the great majority of the learned of those days
regarded the Highland Gaels much as, later on,
Pinkerton and Johnson regarded them, namely

brought his MS. to Douay, where leaves were torn out to
kindle fire in a stove. Lachlan Macmhuirich related that
some of the old parchments at Clanranald's were cut up
by tailors for measuring-tapes (*Rep.,* App., 279).

[1] *The Dean's Book,* p. 125, and the note thereto.

as beings little better than savages, and the
language they spoke merely as a barbarian
dialect. To the remoteness of the Highlands,
and the little intercourse which the inhabitants
held with the outer world, is undoubtedly due
that the language underwent no considerable
variation in the course of centuries.

A few of the poems and ballads have been
preserved to our time in manuscript, and in
Macpherson's time it is not improbable that a
larger number were so extant. But most of
them were preserved by the oral tradition of
the bards. That bards were maintained in all
the great Highland families, that attention and
respect were everywhere paid to them, that
long evenings were spent in listening to their
recitations, is known to every reader of Highland romance. That there would be some
fidelity of tradition among the bards is probable enough ; for much trouble was taken
to preserve the continuity of their order.
The bard lived on his laird's land, which he
held by inheritance, and as a reward for his
services. In some cases it was held on the
special condition that the bard should edu-
cate his children for the same office, so as

to enable the history and poetry connected
with the family to be transmitted from one
generation to another. But while the bards
looked back to Ossian as the head and foun-
tain of their inspiration, and preserved such
poems as were traditionally attributed to him,
they also composed poems of their own. There
can be no manner of doubt that the poems
which were spread over the Highlands, although
they were of a definite character, and related
the exploits of particular heroes, were the outcome of many centuries.

Now there is evidence to show that Macpherson endeavoured not only to collect this poetry,
but also to determine its precise antiquity,[1]
and, more especially, to restore it to its original form. In this he was attempting a task
which the best critic of any age would have
declined. The matter in question was rude,
obscure, and corrupt. It was the production
of a great number of individuals who were
in no kind of contact with one another, but
lived in different ages and in almost complete
isolation. If there was any unity and soli-

---

[1] On this point see the *Report*, 44 ; and the notes appended to *Fingal* and *Temora*, *passim*.

darity to be found in their productions, it was only the unity of the tradition common to them all, that Ossian was the first of their race and the deeds he sung the foremost object of their care. If we suppose that a bard of the name of Ossian composed poems in the third or fourth century, that his poems should have come down pure and unchanged, by oral tradition alone, to the eighteenth century, is not indeed impossible ; but it is incredible. Such tradition for three hundred years has, however, been proved ; for many of the poems obtained by the Highland Society from oral recitation at the beginning of the nineteenth century are substantially the same as poems of the sixteenth preserved in *The Dean's Book.* Doubtless some few poems, regarded as particularly sacred, may have been handed down with little change from remote ages ; but with all their care for these, the bards will have had ambitions of their own. For individual treatment of their theme there was everything to offer the fullest scope, and the quality of the verse naturally varied with the power of the bards. It was in the nature of things that only a few of them could reach a high level ; and it may be taken as certain that half the bombast in the Ossianic poems may be

set down, not to the man who collected and translated them, but to the commonplace qualities of
their ancient authors. In addition to singing the
deeds of Fingal and his heroes, the bards often
celebrated the doings of their own chief and his
clan, which in course of time would inevitably
be mixed up with the ancient theme. On what
grounds, or by what rules, the ancient treatment
of that ancient theme could be distinguished from
other treatments of it less ancient, Macpherson
had no means of determining ; he had none of the
special learning or critical power requisite even
for any approach to the question, and no other
standard to adopt but the general notion that the
better the poetry, and the greater the gap which
it filled in a supposed epic, the purer and more
authentic it was likely to be.

Macpherson undertook his mission at a
critical time in the history of this Highland
poetry ; for it was rapidly disappearing under
the various changes recently introduced by
the English Government. The breakup of
the clan system, the abolition of hereditary jurisdictions, and, above all, the ruin
or exile of many great families which had
participated in the Jacobite risings, brought

about the dispersal of the bards. The language fell into contempt. Adam Ferguson, writing at the end of the century, tells us that the late fashion of the times was to be ignorant of anything written or spoken in Gaelic. It was no longer used at any gentleman's table ; but only by cottagers, herdsmen and deer-stealers. Those who took a pride in their knowledge of it were regarded with suspicion as hostile to Government. There were no books in it but manuals of religion ; and these were written in so awkward and clumsy a style that few could read them.[1] It was only in the remoter districts that the poetry of the language still survived in any quantity. But even there the collector was called upon to make a diligent search ; and what he found was inevitably corrupt.

That Macpherson had undertaken no easy task was fully recognised at the time. Some of the difficulties which he had to encounter were set forth in the very explicit testimony of one of the ministers whom he visited, Dr. John Macpherson, of Knock in Sleat, a man of considerable literary power and strong antiquarian interests, who had excellent opportunities of forming a competent

---

[1] *Rep.*, App., 65.

judgment on the whole matter. The versions given by the several persons who rehearsed the same tales in his presence were, he declared, far from being exactly alike. Some of the rehearsers omitted complete incidents which others had repeated ; some inverted the order of whole sentences and stanzas ; others differed greatly from the rest in expression, here and there in the sentiments, in the versification, in the names of the heroes and scenes of action ; and that, too, without doing any considerable hurt to the merit of the poem.

If such differences could exist between con- temporary versions of the same tales, it is a fact which deserves to be considered by those who complain that the poems in Macpherson's translation are, in tone and temper, unlike poems of undisputed age and authenticity ; for example, that they are unlike the poems in *The Dean's Book.* But between *The Dean's Book* and Macpherson's translation there was an interval of some two hundred and fifty years ; and while a few fragments were collected from oral recitation in the end of the eighteenth century, which differed very little from poems afterwards discovered

in *The Dean's Book,* in many others variety of
treatment would in that long interval necessarily
establish a considerable change of character. To
a still greater extent is this true when we come
to contrast the poems in Macpherson's translation with ancient Irish ballads still extant.
In both cases it is well to remember that, as
we shall see later on, Macpherson treated his
materials with a very free hand.

His criticism, too, was of a very rough and
summary description. A fair specimen of it
is afforded by his attitude towards the Irish
tradition. He was well aware that Ossianic
poetry existed in Ireland, and he took a very
simple course;—he denounced it as spurious. If
he came across any fragments in the Highlands
which seemed to savour of Irish tradition, he
was careful to reject them. [1] He declared [2] that
the bards of Ireland ascribed to Ossian compositions which were evidently their own, and
thus occasioned a general belief in that country
that Fingal was of Irish extraction; whereas in
the poems which he had collected, Fingal was

[1] For two instances of such rejection see his letter given
on p. 152, with the note thereto.
[2] In the preface to *Fingal.*

an ancient Caledonian. The poems which
asserted the contrary were, he said, *ipso facto*
untrustworthy. He maintained that the nature
of the Irish poems and the ignorance of their
authors were sufficiently proved when Ossian
described himself as a contemporary of St.
Patrick, and yet spoke of the Crusades; and
that if a ballad recited in Scotland contained
anything of the same kind, it must be rejected
as Irish. To account for the fact that Ossian
was famous in Ireland as well as in Scotland,
he pointed to the old union between the two
countries; and if the Irish were unaware that
Ossian was Scotch, it was, he declared, simply
because they were ignorant of their own history.

CHAPTER VI.

MACPHERSON'S HIGHLAND MISSION.—THE EVI-
DENCE.—VISITS SKYE AND THE HEBRIDES.—
THE MACMHUIRICHS AND CLANRANALD.—
MANUSCRIPTS.—RETURN TO BADENOCH.

MACPHERSON set out upon his mission towards
the end of August or the beginning of September, 1760.   He was well supplied by his
friends in Edinburgh with letters of introduction
to some of the best known gentry and clergy
in that part of the Highlands which he proposed to visit, and he was everywhere cordially
received.   Home accompanied him, it is said,
for a part of the way.   His first journey was
through the shires of Perth and Argyle to the
north-west district of Inverness.   Thence he
crossed over to the adjacent island of Skye,
and proceeded to the Hebrides, where he visited
North and South Uist and Benbecula.   The
parts of the Highlands which he visited are
just those parts in which, according to many
authorities, the best Gaelic is spoken.

Some account of his travels, and of the way in which he endeavoured to fulfil the object of his mission, is to be obtained from the letters of those whom he encountered in the course of it. These were all, in their various districts, gentlemen of rank, of respectable attainments, and in no wise conspicuous examples of the *perfervidum ingenium Scotorum.* Later on, in common with every one north of the Tweed, they were accused of preferring Scotland to the truth, but they tell the kind of plain tale that bars suspicion. The testimony which they give is evidence, and not mere presumption : it is evidence, too, of first-rate importance ; for they were some of the persons who actually saw Macpherson at work. Three years after his journey, they were called upon to state what they could tell, of their own personal knowledge, of the manner in which he had prosecuted his search, and of the precise nature of the poems which he collected. Whatever opinion may be held of their competence to form a judgment as to the nature of the poems, no one can refuse their evidence regarding the facts of the collection. They have never been seriously accused of dishonesty

anywhere, and in Scotland at least, no charge
of partiality was ever made against any of
them but one ; and in that single case it took
the shape of a mere insinuation on the part
of Macpherson's most pronounced opponent.
The witness in question was a kinsman and
friend, by name Lachlan Macpherson, Laird of
Strathmashie in Badenoch. He accompanied
Macpherson through a part of the Highlands,
and assisted him in collecting fragments.
He himself tells us that he took down
from oral recitation or transcribed from old
manuscripts by far the greater part of the
pieces which Macpherson afterwards published ;
and that he was especially attracted by one of
those manuscripts, written as far back as the
year 1410, which he remembered to have seen
in Macpherson's possession.[1] Let us, however,
set his evidence aside ; although we may do
well to remember that a man is not always a
prophet in his own country, and that the bias
of kinsmen is not always in his favour. But
the possibility of personal bias in any direction

---

[1] *High. Soc. Rep.*, App., 8. Lord Kaimes (*Sketches of Man*, bk. i.) also declared that Macpherson found a Gaelic manuscript in Skye of as old a date as the year 1403.

is certainly a proper reason for excluding testimony, and the exclusion does no harm to the
case. Another informant declares that he understood Macpherson to say that he had obtained
the bulk of his materials in the shires of Perth
and Argyle before he came to the Islands.[1]
This is probably a mistake, and it is in direct
opposition to another statement by a credible
witness.[2] The whole of Macpherson's first journey lasted about six weeks, certainly not more
than two months; and half of this period was
spent in the Islands alone. Of the general conduct of his search there is plenty of evidence
of a perfectly trustworthy character.

As the controversy largely turned on Macpherson's actual proceedings in the Highlands,
it will be desirable to give an account of them
in some detail; more especially as the letters
which supply this account form the chief external
evidence for the general authenticity of the
poems *Fingal* and *Temora*, afterwards published
by him as the result of his search. Direct information of his doings is at hand from the time
when he reached the north-west of Inverness-

[1] *Ibid.*, 97.   [2] *Ibid.*, 176.

shire. At Glenelg, close to that part of the coast
which is separated by a narrow channel from
the Isle of Skye, he paid a visit to Dr. Donald
Macleod, the minister of the place ; and he obtained from him and other persons in the neighbourhood poems or fragments of poems which
Macleod afterwards identified in the text of
Fingal. In particular, he mentioned the description of Cuchullin's horses and car in the
first book as having been taken down at his
own house from the recitation of neighbours.
Further, the battle of Lena in the second book,
parts of the third book, the series of single
combats in the fourth, the fragment relating
the war of Inisthona, and many pieces joined
to other poems in the collection were, he said,
all well known and preserved by tradition in
his country ; besides a great many poems of
similar character, which Macpherson did not
translate.[1] Macpherson, he declared, spent too
little time in the Highlands and Western Isles
to have been able to collect all the poetry of
that district ; and so dispersed was it that
there was no clan all over the Highlands but
possessed some one .specimen that was not to

---

[1] *Ibid.,* 28-30.

be met with anywhere else. That this was no random assertion has been amply shown by the experience of the many other collectors who have been at work since those days. Similar evidence identifying a great many passages in *Fingal* was given by the minister of Sleat,[1] and by other respectable witnesses in the same district.

On his way to the Western Islands Macpherson spent a night in Skinnader in Skye, with a Mr. Alexander Morison. This gentleman, of whom we shall hear more, was afterwards captain of a corps of loyalists in the American War of Independence; he was a good Gaelic scholar, and rendered Macpherson great service in arranging and translating what he found. The next visit recorded was to the Macdonalds of Portree, on the east coast of Skye, whither Macpherson was directed by Dr. Macqueen, minister of Kilmuir, in the northern part of the island. In their house he spent four days and a good part of four nights taking down a variety of poems from one Alexander Macpherson, a smith noted in the country for his knowledge of old poems. The smith, it seems, had good reason to remember

[1] *Ibid.*, 9-12.

the visit ; for he afterwards explained that he was induced to part with a Gaelic manuscript in quarto, procured when he was an apprentice in Lochcarron in Ross-shire, by the expectation which Macpherson held out to him of some future reward ; but that after Macpherson had carried it off, he never heard of it again. The incident was impressed upon his mind all the more deeply because his father, instead of being pleased with the bargain he had made, severely rebuked him for wasting his time.[1]

Macpherson then turned towards the southern part of the Isle of Skye. At Knock, in the district of Sleat, he spent some time with Dr. John Macpherson, who was minister of the district ; and there, perhaps, laid the foundation of a long friendship with the minister's son, afterwards Sir John Macpherson, for a short time Governor-General of India. Like his brother of Glenelg, the minister of Sleat also gave a long list of passages in *Fingal* and the fragments, which, in the original, were commonly recited in his neighbourhood ; and he mentioned the names of those who had recited them in his presence.[2] Some of

[1] *Ibid.*, 92-3. [2] *Ibid.*, 11.

the poems Macpherson obtained from a Captain John Macdonald, who gave his sworn testimony to that effect.[1]　At the same place Macpherson came upon an old acquaintance, Ewen Macpherson, also a native of Badenoch, where, either then or afterwards, he was schoolmaster.　Much against his will, as he reported,[2] he agreed to accompany Macpherson as far as Dunvegan, on the western coast of the island, to assist in the search ; but when he reached Dunvegan, he was, as he quaintly said, " in a manner compulsively obliged " to embark for the Hebrides on the same pursuit.　Besides the poems which Macpherson himself obtained, he received others from Ewen, who went about independently.　Of the two, Ewen was the better acquainted with Gaelic, and he gave Macpherson great assistance.

They landed in Loch Maddy in North Uist, and traversed the Muir to Benbecula.　On

---

[1] Sinclair's edition of the *Poems of Ossian*, i. ccv.

[2] *Rep.*, App., 94-8.　Ewen Macpherson's testimony does not stand on the same footing as that of the other witnesses given in this chapter.　Theirs was contained in letters written not long after the event ; his is a declaration on oath made forty years later.

their way thither they fell in with a man whom
they afterwards found to be John MacCodrum,
a well-known bard in the service of Sir James
Macdonald, himself a youth of great literary
promise. A story is told of their meeting which
illustrates Macpherson's absurd pride and lack of
humour even more than his ignorance of Gaelic.
On asking the bard whether he knew any poems
about the Fingalians, he put the question in
such a way that the words used really meant,
" Do the Fingalians owe you anything ? " Mac-
Codrum, who passed for a wit, took advantage
of the mistake, and humorously replied that if
the Fingalians owed him anything, the bonds
and obligations were lost ; and he believed that
any attempt to recover them at that time of day
would be unavailing. Macpherson, it is said,
took great offence at the sally, and abruptly
went his way.

He spent a week with the younger Clanranald in Benbecula, and from him or through
his agency undoubtedly received several manuscripts of value. This was attested not only by
the Macdonalds themselves and by their bard,
but also by several independent witnesses who
saw them in Macpherson's possession. Clan-

ranald himself declared, in the most positive
terms, that Macpherson had had Gaelic manuscripts from him, and that he did not know
them to exist, until, to gratify his guest, a search
was made amongst the family papers.[1] In South
Uist he met Macmhuirich, the descendant of a
line of bards long in the service of the family;
and one of the last of the order.   Macmhuirich's
son stated that he well remembered Clanranald
making his father give up to Macpherson a
manuscript book written from age to age by his
ancestors, who were thus preserving the history
of the Macdonalds and other Highland clans,
and that the book contained some of the works
of Ossian and other bards.

According to the account which he gave,[2] the
son described himself as eighteenth in descent
from Muireach, the progenitor of his family.   He
gave his evidence in the year 1800.   If we allow
three generations to a century, Muireach would
have flourished about the year 1200.   Now
poems by this Muireach or Murdoch, and by
other members of the same family, appear in

[1] *Rep.*, pp. 36, 80.
[2] *Ibid.*, App., 278.

The Dean's Book.[1] By all that we can learn of
Muireach, he seems to have come over from Ireland, where he was a well-known poet. O'Curry,
in his great work on the *Manners and Customs of
the Ancient Irish,* cites a passage from the *Annals
of the Four Masters,* set down under the date
1213, in which the circumstances attending his
flight to Scotland are recorded in some detail.[2]

[1] Ed. M'Lauchlan, pp. 108, 112, 157, 158.

[2] O'Curry, *op. cit.,* iii. 280. " Finn O'Brodlachain,
steward to the O'Donnell, that is O'Donnell Mór (prince of
Tir-Chonnail), went into Connaught to collect O'Donnell's
rent. The first place that he went to was *Cairpre* of Drum-
cliffe. He then went with his attendants to the house of
Muireadhach O'Daly, of Lissadill, where he fell to offering
great abuse to the poet, for he was very exacting on behalf
of a powerful man (not that it was his master that advised
him to it). The poet was incensed by him, and he took up
a keen-edged hatchet in his hand, and gave him a blow
which left him dead without life. He went then himself to
avoid O'Donnell into Clanrickard's country." The *Annals*
go on to relate that Muireach was pursued by O'Donnell
through Thomond to Limerick and thence to Dublin, and
from Dublin was forced to flee to Scotland ; and that when
he was there he composed three laudatory poems imploring
peace, forgiveness, and protection from O'Donnell. O'Curry
states that none of these three poems were known to be
extant in Ireland, but that two of them are preserved in
the Bodleian Library at Oxford in the vellum MS. containing
O'Donnell's life of St. Columba; further, that the account
given by the *Four Masters* in certain particulars probably

It is obvious that if this Irish descent of
the Macmhuirichs is well established, it has a
very significant bearing on some of the issues
raised in the Ossianic controversy. And that the
Macmhuirichs, even in Macpherson's day, were
known to be connected with Ireland is evident
from what we are told by the minister of Sleat.
The minister knew the bard to be a man
of some letters; "that is to say, he and his
ancestors for many ages had received their education in Irish colleges of poetry and history,
and understood the Latin tolerably well ".[1]   He
affirmed, further, that about the year 1733,
he had seen one of the Macmhuirichs travelling
about through the Highlands and Isles with a
Gaelic manuscript, out of which he read, before
him and many others, the exploits of Cuchullin,
Fingal, Ossian, Oscar, Gaul, Dermid, and other
heroes; and that the last of the Macmhuirichs,
to his certain knowledge, possessed several
manuscripts in verse as well as prose.[2]

partakes more of tradition than of historic fact.   He also
states that Muireach, when he fled to Scotland, seems to
have found shelter and protection from Clanranald; and
the statement is doubtless based on the presence of poems
by Muireach in *The Dean's Book.*

[1] *Rep.*, App., 6.
[2] *Ibid.*, 10.

There was some difference of opinion as regards the name of the book which Macmhuirich gave to Macpherson. Ewen Macpherson, present when it was delivered, recorded his strong opinion that the book then given was not, as Macmhuirich stated, the *Leabhar Dearg*, or *Red Book*, which was highly esteemed in that part of the Highlands as containing ancient poetry; but that Macpherson obtained an order for the *Red Book* from Clanranald on Donald Macdonald of Edinburgh.[1] A Mr. Angus Macneill, minister of Hovemore in South Uist, gave a different account of the book obtained in Edinburgh. It was, as Clanranald had expressly declared to him, a transcript he had made from a large manuscript treating of the wars of Fingal and Comhal his father, the original of which had been carried off to Ireland, where it disappeared. Macneill declared that two of his parishioners recited several pieces of ancient verse which agreed without any material variation with passages in Macpherson's rendering in the second, fourth and fifth books of *Fingal*, and that the original of *Berrathon*, the last of the poems appended to *Fingal*, was contained in an

[1] *Ibid.*, 97.

9

important manuscript which, with three or four more, Macmhuirich in his presence gave to Macpherson, who bound himself in writing to return them.

There is evidence to show that Macpherson parted very reluctantly with whatever he had succeeded in obtaining. Blair said that when he was in the Highlands in 1772, several of the gentlemen who had supplied Macpherson with manuscripts complained of his still keeping them, notwithstanding solemn promises and notes of hand. The smith at Portree was loud in his complaints on this head, and even the Macdonalds themselves had some difficulty in getting back the manuscripts which Sir James had lent. They were the more anxious to do so, as some of these papers contained a good deal of the family history. After some ineffectual correspondence they directed an action to be brought for their recovery. We learn that the action was stayed, and that Macpherson bound himself to return them as soon as he had accomplished his purpose.[1] This he probably did; for on his

---

[1] *Rep.*, 81.

death only one small and unimportant volume was found by his executors.[1]

The search in the Hebrides was brought to an end with the visit to the Macdonalds, and Macpherson then turned towards his native valleys, partly to collect further materials, partly to enlist the services of one or two friends in an examination of what he had found. For this purpose he spent some time on his way to Ruthven with a missionary in Brae-Badenoch, the Rev. Andrew Gallie, who many years afterwards gave a valuable account of the meeting.[2] He well remembered, he said, that when Macpherson arrived at his house he brought out several old volumes, much worm-

---

[1] It was on the *Red Book* that the family probably set the most store ; and it was returned, for it is now in their possession. A gentleman who has lately examined it informs me that Macmhuirich's statement that it contained the history of the Macdonalds and other Highland clans, together with some poems, is perfectly correct. The history dates from the earliest times up to the reign of James VII. ; it includes an interesting account, by an eye-witness, of the doings of the Highland host in Montrose's wars, and it is interspersed with poems, which are for the most part elegies on departed chiefs. Campbell of Islay, who examined it in 1873, declared that he found no poem in it which could be the original of any part of Macpherson's *Ossian*.

[2] *Rep.*, 30-43.

eaten and otherwise injured by time. They
were written in the Gaelic language and character, and contained poems alleged to be the
work of Ossian and other ancient bards. Many
of these old volumes had all the appearance of
monkish origin : not only were the characters
beautiful and the spelling correct, but the text
was everywhere illuminated and the initial
words coloured and flourished. They were
written on a material that seemed like coarse
vellum, and strongly bound in parchment. These
volumes were, as Macpherson declared, among
those given to him by Clanranald ; and some of
them contained a statement at the end, to the
effect that they were collected by Paul Macmhuirich, the bard of the family at the beginning of the fourteenth century.

We will not scrutinise the date too closely ;
but apart from that, Gallie's evidence is no less
valuable than curious. When it was first published, there were few, perhaps, who would have
accepted it without a smile of suspicion ; and
the controversialist had a fine opportunity of
ridiculing a claim to authenticity on the part of
poems alleged to be Ossianic, but derived from
an ecclesiastical source. Yet if anything at all

has been clearly established by the labours of Gaelic scholars since then, it is that the most ancient Gaelic poetry was preserved by the hand of priests and missionaries. Of that fact *The Dean's Book* alone is irrefutable testimony. Nay more : some of the poems there given under the name of Murdoch Albanach,[1] who is the Muireach previously mentioned, are of a religious character. It will hardly be pretended that Macpherson knew of the existence of *The Dean's Book*, or was competent to manufacture worm-eaten parchments of ecclesiastical writing and illumination ; or that if he had attempted any such imposture, he could have succeeded in imposing upon the credulity of his friends in Edinburgh. He was anxious to establish that the Ossianic poetry was of pre-Christian origin ; he may have even suppressed some passages in his version to give colour to this contention ; but if he had been a mere forger, parchments of an ecclesiastical character were the last thing that he would be likely to produce.

[1] See *The Dean's Book*, p. 157, and M'Lauchlan's note. Murdoch appears to have held some ecclesiastical office.

CHAPTER VII.

MACPHERSON'S MATERIALS.—HIS METHOD.—HIS
    KNOWLEDGE OF GAELIC.—THE TRANSLATION.
    —HIS SECOND JOURNEY.—RETURNS TO EDIN-
    BURGH.—PROPOSAL TO PUBLISH THE ORIGI-
    NALS.—RAMSAY'S ACCOUNT OF HIM.

UNLESS we are to believe that the witnesses
quoted in the preceding chapter, many of whom
had no acquaintance with one another and
dwelt in districts far apart, were all in a conspiracy to lie for the benefit of a man previously
unknown to them, it is impossible to doubt that
Fingal, *Temora*, and the various *Fragments*
which Macpherson published, were in a large
measure versions of poems commonly recited in
the Highlands. It is also certain that besides
what he gathered from oral recitation, Macpherson obtained a number of manuscripts, and
was known to have obtained them before a line
of *Fingal* or *Temora* appeared. This is clearly
established by the undisputed testimony of those
who gave him the manuscripts, or saw him receive
them, or saw them in his possession. He had

shown them to Gallie, and he brought them under the notice of his literary friends in Edinburgh, some of whom were the best scholars of the day.

While the chief part of what he collected was taken down from oral recitation, it is highly probable that these manuscripts also furnished him with some of his material. Gallie affirmed that there were poems in the ecclesiastical parchments which he read. Dr. Macleod, Professor of Church History at Glasgow, reported to Lord Bannatyne that . he had seen and examined several Gaelic manuscripts in Macpherson's possession, partly written on vellum and apparently of great antiquity ; and that they consisted of poems mixed up with other compositions. Nor is it difficult to form a reasonable conjecture as to the character of the volumes obtained from the Macdonalds and other families. It was among the bards' duties to preserve the history and genealogy of the families to which they were attached ; and such of their chronicles as have survived to this day are found to contain scraps of old poetry mingled with the narrative. That some of the documents which Macpherson

secured were of this nature is proved by the
contemptuous statement of one of his most
acrimonious critics, to whom, many years afterwards, they were privately shown.   He declared
that, so far as he could see, the alleged originals
were only old Irish and Highland genealogies.[1]
Finally, Macpherson himself admitted to one
of his correspondents[2] that the old manuscripts
which he had discovered were only in part
poetical.

He treated his materials with a very free
hand, much, indeed, after the fashion in which
Percy, a year or two later, treated his *Reliques
of Ancient English Poetry.*   For abundant evidence on this head the reader may turn to
the Report of the Highland Society,[3] where a
number of Gaelic poems, as they were then
commonly recited in the North, are printed
side by side with a literal rendering and the
translation given by Macpherson.   Good ex-

---

[1] See Shaw's *Inquiry into the Authenticity of the Poems
ascribed to Ossian,* p. 84.   For other instances where religious and genealogical literature was found to contain an
admixture of Gaelic poetry, see accounts given by Lord
Bannatyne, *Rep.,* App., 282, and *ibid.,* 290.

[2] See *infra,* p. 147.

[3] App., 189-260.

ternal testimony to the same effect is supplied by Gallie's statement, together with that of Captain Morison and the Laird of Strathmashie, who assisted Macpherson at this time, and saw how he treated his materials.[1] The manuscripts were not easy reading; they were written in the old character, which gave Macpherson, it is clear, no small trouble; and even Gallie, though a fair scholar, made it out with difficulty. Strathmashie, however, was very well acquainted with the language; and he helped the translator in piecing the fragments together and in writing them out in Roman character. On his death in 1767, a manuscript is said to have been found amongst his papers, containing the Gaelic of the seventh book of *Temora* in his handwriting, with numerous alterations and corrections, and headed, " First rude draft of· the seventh book of Temora ".[2] We can thus form a notion of the

[1] *Rep.*, 33, and App., 177.

[2] *The Dean's Book*, Skene's Introd., lvii. There is no evidence to show the precise date previous to 1767 at which the draft was written; but it is worth mentioning that it was the Gaelic of the seventh book which was published with *Temora* in the beginning of the year 1763, as a specimen of the original.

way in which the Gaelic original was composed.

Gallie declared that the manuscripts were
so worn and decayed that words and even
whole lines were illegible ; and he supplied
an important piece of information when he
said that for these illegible passages Macpherson was very clever in substituting others
of his own ; which, if they did not recover the
exact words and ideas of Ossian, were no
discredit to that bard. Similar evidence was
given by Morison, who left on record that he
had often to copy out the Gaelic, as Macpherson
was unable to write or spell it ; that he gave
him much assistance in translating ; and that
it was their general practice, when any passage
occurred which they did not understand, either
to leave it out, or to gloss it over with any
expression that might appear to fit in with
the context.[1]   Morison further declared that
while Macpherson was deserving of great praise
for collecting the poems and for arranging them,
he had little original ability, and could no more
have composed the Ossianic poems, or anything

[1] See Graham's *Essay on the Authenticity of Ossian's
Poems*, p. 284.

like them, than he could have written the
prophecies of Isaiah or created the Island of
Skye; and that so far from possessing a competent knowledge even of the language in
which they were handed down, he was often
at a loss to understand the very meaning of
the words.

We know already that Macpherson had
a poor knowledge of the language; and
Gallie's statement not only confirms this, but
shows us that in spite of his deficiencies,
Macpherson had a good opinion of himself.
He argued with his host about the significance
of various phrases; and that their disputes
ran high may be inferred from the fact that
Mrs. Gallie remembered them at a distance of
forty years. He also took upon himself to
determine the authorship of the poems by
internal evidence; and according to Gallie,
swore freely whenever he came upon any
passages in which he thought that the bard
who was reciting Ossian's poems had ventured
to introduce compositions of his own.[1]

[1] For another instance in which Macpherson is said to
have suspected the modernity of a poem recited to him
as ancient, see the *Report*, p. 58.

It is obvious, of course, that Macpherson's productions were built up out of fragments. Gallie declined to say that Macpherson found *Fingal* arranged as he gave it to the public; nor did any of those who saw him at work collecting or translating offer any evidence to that effect. He spent his time in Badenoch in fitting poems together, and preparing the material for a connected translation. He unquestionably thought that the fragments which he found could be restored to their place in that ancient epic which he, in common with Blair, honestly believed to have existed. On a fair view of the evidence it is obvious that many of the witnesses knew perfectly well that Macpherson did not find his epic entire, but composed it out of short poems. For instance, Mr. Macqueen, minister of Kilmuir, who was in communication with the Macdonalds, and rendered Macpherson good service, declared his belief that the work was put together in that fashion, and that for every part of it there was a foundation in the ancient songs.[1] This was also the opinion of Adam Ferguson,[2] who maintained that, after all, Homer had done nothing

---

[1] *Ibid.*, 36.   [2] *Ibid.*, 64.

else. It is not unlikely that for the amplification of obscure references to manners and customs he borrowed freely from Toland's *History of the Druids.* That Macpherson produced his epic in some such way, and, further, that he softened many of the incidents by refining the language, and supplied connections where they were wanting, was the conclusion reached by the Highland Society, after a long inquiry conspicuous for its moderation and fairness. To some extent he admitted that he supplied connections ; for when Dr. MacIntyre of Glenorchay accused him of interpolation, he replied : " I had occasion to do less of that than you suppose ".[1] That the translations which he published were either wholly, or in a large measure, based upon a very free use of his material, is an hypothesis which supplies a better explanation of a larger number of the facts than any other that can be adduced. In the face of the evidence, it is impossible to believe that he forged the whole of the translation ; and, on the other hand, it is equally impossible to believe that every line of it was taken from a Gaelic original.

[1] Sinclair's ed. of the *Poems of Ossian,* iii. 465.

Although he claimed for his translation that it was literal, it was, in fact, scarcely more than a paraphrase. It is certain that if he had failed to treat his materials with a free hand, after the fashion of the times, his version would have met with no success. But there were serious complaints of his freedom. Most of those who identified passages in *Fingal* and *Temora*, or in the pieces affixed to them, with poems which they had heard recited in their own districts, were strongly of opinion that these poems had suffered in Macpherson's hands. Two or three of the witnesses declared, with Morison, that when he came upon a passage which he did not understand, he omitted it ; that in particular the description of Cuchullin's horses and car in the first book of *Fingal* had been in this way seriously mutilated.[1] The minister of Glenelg complained that Macpherson had omitted a description of Fingal's ships, their yards, masts, and rigging, their extraordinary feats in sailing, and the skill and courage of the men ; and he accounted for the omission by the fact that the translator was born in an inland part of the kingdom, and having no acquaintance with sea-

[1] *Rep.*, App., 29, 32, 77.

manship did not perhaps understand the original.[1] Others were of opinion that upon the whole he had done his work as well as the genius of the language would allow, and that no other version was any better.

In endeavouring to reconcile various versions of the same poem, or to prefer one version to another, Macpherson was well within his rights as an editor; and that he exercised his judgment with great freedom is everywhere apparent from the notes which he appended to his translation. He also modified many of the proper names, out of a regard for English ears, and English ignorance of the liquid sound of the Gaelic language; nor is it improbable that he obtained some of the names from Toland's *History*, and that he invented others.

Critics have often said in their haste that the genuine Gaelic poetry which survives from the sixteenth century, to mention no earlier date, exhibits none of the elegance of Macpherson's work. It must be obvious to all but fanatics, that not only some of the

[1] *Ibid.*, 31. For abundant examples of the way in which Macpherson is said to have misunderstood or misrepresented the original, see Sinclair's *op. cit.*, i. 95.

elegance, but some also of the refined sentiment, which pervades *Fingal, Temora,* and the
Fragments, is due to the kind of language which
Macpherson used in those works, partly under
the influence of the taste prevailing in his day,
and partly as a tribute to it. His reluctance
to undertake a search at all was, it will be remembered, re-inforced by the fear which he held
out, that the rough poetry of the Highlands
would hardly fit in with modern ideas of culture
and refinement. If his versions were polished
out of all resemblance to the originals, it was
the taste of the day which was chiefly at fault ;
for it was a day when Pope's paraphrase of
Homer was regarded as a model of elegant
translation. But no candid and competent
person can read such Gaelic poems of the sixteenth century as are preserved in *The Dean's
Book* without perceiving that much of the
pathos and refinement which forms so striking
a feature of Macpherson's productions is
equally conspicuous there ; [1] that there, too, the

---

[1] See the melancholy lines attributed to Ossian, pp.
3 *et seq.* See also pp. 20, 34, 43, 54-7. If these poems were
freely rendered into measured prose in the style of *Carthon.*
they would make a very fair addition to Macpherson's work,

heroes sometimes exhibit that magnanimous character which astonished Macpherson's contemporaries. They are terrible in war, but just,
generous and faithful to their friends. There is
the same delight in the chase, the same joy in the
sound of battle, the same desolation in defeat,
the same mourning for the dead. The women,
too, play as large and as important a part as in
Fingal or *Temora;* their charms are sung with
as great an enthusiasm, their modesty is as celebrated, they bemoan the fate of their lovers and
the death of the brave with as passionate a grief.
It has been said that the scenery as well as the
sentiment of the Ossianic poems is Macpherson's
own ; but in *The Dean's Book* we find similar
mention of clouds, mountains, valleys and streams,
and similar metaphors drawn from the rush and
tumult of the sea. The descriptive colouring is
equally strong, and the epithets are equally bold :
the heroes' eyes are blue, their skin is white, their
cheeks and lips are red, their locks are black or
yellow. If none of the poems in the older
collection are identical with those embedded
in Macpherson's epics, it is undeniable that
many of the characteristic features of both are
the same.

10

Macpherson collected what he could in
Badenoch ; and he wrote to several gentlemen
elsewhere to make inquiries. Some of his
letters to a Mr. James McLagan, minister of
Amulrie in Perthshire,[1] have been preserved.

" Ruthven, 27th October, 1760.

" Reverend Sir,

" You perhaps have heard that I am employed to make a collection of the ancient poetry
in the Gaelic. I have already traversed most
of the Isles, and gathered all worth notice in
that quarter. I intend a journey to Mull and
the coast of Argyle to enlarge my collection.

"By letters from Edinburgh, as well as gentlemen of your acquaintance, I am informed that
you have a good collection of poems of the kind
I want. It would be, therefore, very obliging,
you should transmit me them as soon as convenient, that my book might be rendered more
complete and more for the honour of our old
poetry. Traditions are uncertain ; poetry delivered down from memory must lose considerably ;
and it is a matter of surprise to me how we have
now any of the beauties of our ancient Gaelic
poetry remaining.

" Your collection, I am informed, is pure, as
you have taken pains to restore the style. I
shall not make any apology for this trouble, as
it will be for the honour of our ancestors how
many of their pieces of genius are brought to
light. I have met with a number of old manu-

[1] *Rep.*, App., 153.

scripts in my travels; the poetical part of them
I have endeavoured to secure.

"If anything of that kind falls within your
hearing, I beg it of you to have them in sight.

"I shall probably do myself the pleasure of
waiting of you before I return to Edinburgh.
Your correspondence in the meantime will be
very agreeable. You will excuse this trouble
from an entire stranger; and believe me,

"Reverend Sir,

"Your most humble servant,

"JAMES MACPHERSON.

"Inform me what you can of the tradition of
the poems. Direct to me, by Edinburgh and
Ruthven, enclosed to Mr. Macpherson, post-
master here."

In reply to this request McLagan sent several
detached pieces; in particular, some passages in
the two last books of *Fingal*, the poem called
Erragon, or the Battle of Lorn, and a fragment
which bears some resemblance to the opening of
Temora.[1]

On leaving Ruthven Macpherson made his
second journey. Of this there is hardly any
record. He went to the coast of Argyleshire
and to Mull. On his way thither, he stayed
in Glenorchay, at the house of a Mr. M'Vean,

[1] *Ibid.*, 24.

a minister, and there heard recitations from one John M'Nicol of Arivean, of a family which had for ages been celebrated for reciting songs and poems. The person who gave the information declared that he was well acquainted with a large number of Ossianic poems which he had heard recited in different parts of the Highlands long before Macpherson came to Glenorchay, and he laid particular stress on the poem translated under the title of *Darthula*, and annexed to *Fingal*.[1]

Macpherson had now spent some four months upon his mission. From time to time he had,

---

[1] The tale of *Darthula* is well known. It is common to Ireland and Scotland, and various versions of it are to be found in extant MSS. in both countries. In Macpherson's day it was also rehearsed orally in Glenelg, Sleat, and elsewhere in the Highlands. The minister of Hovemore (*Rep.*, App., 20) stated that Macmhuirich had repeated before him the edition which Macpherson had obtained from that bard. According to Skene, the oldest Scottish version of it is in the Glenmasan papers, now in the collection of Gaelic MSS. in the Advocates' Library at Edinburgh. It bears the date of 1238. Dr. Angus Smith, in his *Loch Etive and the Sons of Uisnach*, connects many passages in the poem, as Macpherson gave it, with the neighbourhood of *Loch Etive*. A more ambitious attempt to settle the topography of the Ossianic poems, and indirectly to establish their authenticity, has been made by Dr. Hately Waddell in his large work *Ossian and the Clyde*.

as Blair records,[1] written to his literary friends
to inform them of the success of his search. In
the early days of January, 1761, he returned to
Edinburgh, laden with his poetical treasures, and
took lodgings immediately below Blair's house at
the head of Blackfriars' Wynd.

It was thus, almost under the eye of the
most conspicuous literary personage in Edinburgh, and in the constant company of the
circle which gathered at his house, that Macpherson continued the translation which he
had begun in Badenoch. It is highly probable that Blair assisted him in arranging the
poems and in polishing the English version.
He had already shown a very strong interest
in the work; and now, as he tells us, he saw
Macpherson frequently, and induced him to
read or repeat parts of the translation as he
wrote it. Home, it seems, had done something of the same kind in the case of the
Fragments.[2] It was probably to the assist-

---

[1] *Rep.*, App., 59.

[2] In Baker's *Biog. Dram.*, i. 362, it is stated that Macpherson left Home £2000. There is no mention of such
a legacy in the copy of his will in Somerset House; but
the statement may refer to a donation. Macpherson appears

ance of these eminent men of letters that some
of the success of Macpherson's work was due;
and to the same source we may perhaps look
for an explanation of the difficulty which Gray
felt when he expressed his astonishment that
the translations should have been the work of
a man whose private letters at the time were
" ill-wrote and ill-reasoned ". It is also probable that his friends helped him to gather
facts and arguments for that critical dissertation on the antiquity of the poems, by which
he endeavoured to give a scholarly tone to the
work. Into this he collected all the references
to Celtic tradition which could be found in
ancient writers; and, after a fashion not
unknown in the study of antiquity in any
age, he supplemented them by free guesses
of his own. He also appended a great many
notes of a quasi-historical and critical character;
and by quoting passages from well-known
authors, ancient and modern, which bore some
resemblance to passages in the old poems, or to
particular phrases in his version of them, he

to have been of a grateful temper and sincerely attached to
his friends, and he may have pressed a sum of money upon
Home in recognition of his services.

boldly challenged a comparison with works of established reputation.

By his own admission Blair knew nothing of Gaelic, and never looked into Macpherson's papers. Several other scholars, however, including Adam Ferguson, reported that they had examined the old manuscripts, and that on comparing the translation with any parts of the original which they read, they were satisfied of its accuracy.[1] Ferguson added that the fragments which he had seen " by no means appeared of recent writing; the papers were much stained with smoke, and daubed with Scots snuff ".[2]

Macpherson continued to receive poems from his friends in the Highlands, as appears by the following letter, written at this period, and also addressed to his correspondent at Amulrie.

[1] The names of the other scholars are not recorded. While Ferguson doubtless saw the manuscripts in Macpherson's possession, the original which he compared with the translation was probably the transcript made in Roman character by Macpherson's friends in Badenoch. Some thirty years later, in a letter to Macpherson, dated 30th May, 1793, Ferguson spoke of himself as " a bastard Gaelic man," and of " the barbarous orthography which few, and I among the rest, never learned to read " (Small's *Biographical Sketch of Adam Ferguson,* p. 56).

[2] *Rep.,* App., 59.

Out of the materials which were now collected he had composed something that in
his own opinion, and in the opinion of his
friends, looked like an epic, complete with
main subject, episodes, and methodical divi-
sion into books; and he began to speak of
it as on a level with other great epics. In
this he was doubtless confirmed by Blair,
who afterwards wrote an elaborate dissertation to prove that in many respects Ossian
was superior to Homer.

"Edinburgh, 16th January, 1761.

" I was favoured with your letter enclosing
the Gaelic poems, for which I hold myself extremely obliged to you. *Duan a Ghairibb*[1] is
less poetical and more obscure than *Teantach mor
na Feinne.* The last is far from being a bad poem,
were it complete, and is particularly valuable for
the ancient manners it contains. I shall reckon

---

[1] Macpherson afterwards spoke of *Duan a Ghairibb* in
the preface to *Temora* as an Irish poem, which he had
thought of translating. It was, he said, of some grandeur,
but contained several low and indecent passages. It is
a curious and noteworthy fact that, in the same place, he
also quotes a verse from *Teantach mor na Feinne*, in which
St. Patrick is mentioned, and reference made to a pilgrim-
age to the Holy Land, *viz.*, the Crusades. On these grounds
he rejects Irish traditional poetry, which, as this letter shows,
was known in the Highlands at the time of his journey.

myself much obliged to you for any other pieces
you can send me. It is true I have the most of
them from other hands ; but the misfortune is that
I find none expert in the Irish orthography, so
that an obscure poem is rendered doubly so by
their uncouth way of spelling. It would have
given me real pleasure to have got your letter
before I left the Highlands, as in that case I
would have done myself the pleasure of waiting
of you, but I do not despair but something may
cast up, that may bring about an interview ; as I
have some thoughts of making a jaunt to Perthshire. Be that, however, as it will, I shall always
be glad of your correspondence, and hope that
you will give me all convenient assistance in my
present undertaking.

"I have been lucky enough to lay my hands on
a pretty complete poem, and truly epic, concerning Fingal. The antiquity of it is easily ascertained, and it is not only superior to anything in
that language, but reckoned not inferior to the
more polite performances of other nations in that
way. I have some thoughts of publishing the
original, if it will not clog the work too much.

" I shall be always ready to acknowledge the
obligation you have laid upon me, and promise I
will not be ungrateful for further favours. It
would give me pleasure to know how I can serve
you."

It will be observed that Macpherson here
made no secret of his difficulties in dealing
with the language ; and he tacitly admitted that
he had to seek assistance in deciphering the old
aracter. But amongst his friends in Edinburgh

there was doubtless some desire that he should
publish the originals, and he showed himself
anxious to accede to their wishes.   He had
already told McLagan that he entertained some
idea of the kind, and he wrote to him on the
subject again.

"Edinburgh, 8th February, 1761.

"I am favoured with your last letter, enclosing four poems, for which I am obliged to
you.   I beg you send me what more you can
conveniently.   I have resolved to print by subscription.   I send, enclosed, a copy of my proposals, that if any in your neighbourhood incline
to subscribe, they send their orders, by your
means, to me, and I shall send signed receipt,
and take care to convey the book when published.   I am now much hurried, so that I have
scarce time to thank you for your readiness to
answer my demands."

The proposal fell through for lack of support.
Macpherson afterwards prefixed an advertisement to his translation, informing the public of
the motives which had induced him to depart
from his intention.   Some men of genius, he
said, whom he had the honour to number among
his friends, had advised him to publish the
originals, as a better way of satisfying scruples
as to their authenticity than by depositing ma^r

scripts in a public library. He issued his proposal, but as no subscriber appeared he concluded that the public did not require either the one course or the other. However, he spoke of his intention to publish the originals himself, as soon as he should have time to transcribe them for the press; and if the publication did not, after all, take place, he declared that he would deposit copies in one of the public libraries.

Ramsay, whose notes furnished some of the facts in an earlier chapter of the narrative, tells us of a visit which he paid to Macpherson in the early part of this year, in company with Robert Chalmers. He found him living at the back of the Guard, in a small room full of books and manuscripts. Some of the manuscripts bore, he reported, evident marks of antiquity. One of them Macpherson described as an old Gaelic book on medicine, by an *Ollah*, or Highland doctor.[1] The impression which

[1] Macpherson obviously meant *Ollamh* (pron. *Ollave*), a name indicating the highest rank in the learned professions of ancient Ireland (see O'Curry, *Manners and Customs of the Ancient Irish*, ii., 78, 172, and iii., 52, 53). That Macpherson found, or professed to have found, any such book in the Highlands is a fact of great significance.

Ramsay obtained of Macpherson himself was that he was a plain-looking lad, dressed like a preacher ; and that, while his conversation was sensible, his manner was starched and reserved.

CHAPTER VIII.

GOES TO LONDON. — INTRODUCTIONS. — BUTE, HORACE WALPOLE.—PROTEST FROM IRELAND.—PUBLICATION OF " FINGAL ".—EXTRACTS.

IT is obvious that when the poems passed for the composition of a Scottish Homer in the third century, whose song had been marvellously preserved for fifteen hundred years, their publication was regarded as a literary event of the first importance. The fame of it led the way. After the fashion of the times the book was to be issued by subscription ; and while Blair and his friends may have been anxious that a work so flattering to the national pride should appear in Edinburgh, they looked to London to fill the list. For in London there was another Scotchman even greater than Blair, and still more conspicuous, who took a strong interest in the enterprise, and, moreover, was ready to use his influence on behalf of it. The Earl of Bute, who had become a powerful Minister on the accession

of George III., was then and always distinguished by his generous patronage of literature,[1] and he naturally extended his protection to a young countryman with whose friends
Home and Adam Ferguson he was intimate.   It
was probably at Bute's suggestion that it was
decided to publish the work in London.

Accordingly, in the early spring of 1761,
Macpherson left Edinburgh in order to superin-
tend the printing.   Robert Chalmers was his
companion on the journey.   It is not recorded
where he lodged when he first arrived in
London ; but he brought good introductions.
Hume, for instance, gave him the following
letter to William Strahan, the publisher :—

"Edinburgh, 9th February, 1761.
"Dear Sir,
"I cannot give you a better return for your
obliging Letter than by introducing to your Acquaintance the Bearer, Mr. M'Pherson, who
translated some Fragments of Highland Poetry,
which have been extremely well received by the
Public, and have probably come to your hands.
He has also translated a larger Work, a Narrative
Poem of great Antiquity, which lay in Obscurity,
would probably have been bury'd in Oblivion,
if he had not retrieved it.   He proposes to print

[1] It was Bute who gave Johnson a pension in 1762.

it by Subscription, and his Friends here are very busy in procuring him Encouragement. He goes up to London with the same intention ; and you may readily believe, that I advis'd him to think of nobody but our Friend, Mr. Millar, in disposing of the Copy. He will probably need your Advice in several Particulars ; and as he is an entire stranger in London, you will naturally of yourself be inclin'd to assist him. He is also very worthy of your Friendship ; being a sensible, modest young Fellow, a very good Scholar, and of unexceptionable Morals. I have advis'd him to be at first on a Footing of Confidence with you ; and hope you will receive him as one who merits your Friendship.

" I am, dear Sir,

" Your most obedient Servant,

" DAVID HUME."

Macpherson found himself an object of interest to the literary circles of London ; and his work was awaited there with as much eagerness as in Edinburgh. The *Fragments* were reprinted by Dodsley,[1] and parts of the new translation were handed about in manuscript. The first book of *Fingal* was sent to Horace Walpole, probably by the translator

[1] On April 14, 1761, Macpherson received ten guineas from Dodsley for the right of printing a new edition. See catalogue of the sale of Mr. Lewis Pocock's *Johnsoniana*, May, 1875. (Copy in *Brit. Mus.*)

himself. Writing on 14th April, Walpole expressed his high admiration of its beautiful
images and its natural sentiment. He noted
more especially that there was none of that
particularisation of the persons, that frequent
recurrence of *he said*, and *he replied*, which
deformed Homer ; but to avoid confusion he
had, as he informed his correspondent, advised
Macpherson to have the names prefixed to the
persons, as in a play. This Macpherson did,
wherever he thought it necessary. Walpole
declared that all his doubts on the score of
authenticity had completely vanished.

In Ireland it was not interest so much as
suspicion, and even anger, that was aroused
by Macpherson's work. The rumour that the
poems of Ossian, an ancient Highland bard,
were about to be published by a Scotchman,
had, of course, reached that country. The Irish
declared that the Scotchman was stealing their
national heroes ; and before a line of the poems
was published, there came a singular protest
from Dublin, in the shape of an advertisement
earnestly entreating the public to wait for a
version of the deeds of Fingal which would at
least be genuine. It does not appear that any

such version was published, or that anything
came of the protest, which on the face of it
was only meant to be mischievous.[1]

The first part of Macpherson's translations
was published in London in the beginning of
December, 1761,[2] and a few days later in Edinburgh. Those who are curious in such matters
may be pleased to know that it was brought out

[1] The advertisement, inserted in *Faulkner's Dublin Journal* for 1st December, 1761, was in the following terms :
" Speedily will be published by a gentleman of this kingdom,
who hath been, for some time past, employed in translating
and writing Historical Notes to it, FINGAL, A POEM. Originally wrote in the Irish or Erse language. In the preface to
which, the translator, who is a perfect master of the Irish
tongue, will give an account of the manners of the antient
Irish or Scotch ; and therefore most humbly intreats the
public to wait for his edition, which will appear in a short
time, as he will set forth all the blunders and absurdities
in the edition now printing in London, and show the ignorance of the English translator, in his knowledge of Irish
grammar, not understanding any part of that accidence."

[2] Walpole's *Letters*, iii. 466   See also Boswell's *Correspondence with the Hon. A. Erskine*, ed. Dr. Birkbeck Hill,
under the dates 16th and 17th December, 1761.   It is
always stated that *Fingal* appeared in 1762, which is the
date on the title-page of the first edition ; but this is explained by the common practice of publishers, then and
now, in the case when a book is issued in the last few
weeks of the year, to describe it as appearing in the next
year.

in quarto form by Becket and De Hondt, well-
known publishers in the Strand, and that it sold
for half a guinea. It bore the following title :
*Fingal, an Ancient Epic Poem, in Six Books ;
together with several other Poems, composed by
Ossian, the Son of Fingal. Translated from the
Galic Language by James Macpherson.* The
translator contributed a Preface, narrating the
circumstances which led to the publication, and
giving an outline of the story told in the epic.
In the advertisement he expressed himself
deeply sensible of the generosity of a certain
noble person, whom he avoided to name,
"as his exalted station as well as merit had
raised him above the panegyric of one so little
known ".

There is much in the work that time has not
wholly robbed of the power to charm ; and to
give a few further examples of its style may be
no unwelcome digression to those who have
never read " the poems of Ossian ". The critic
will have his own pleasure in contrasting them
with the extracts already given from Macpherson's early poetry. The following passages from
Fingal illustrate the descriptions of battle scattered through the work.

"As the dark shades of autumn fly over hills of grass; so gloomy, dark, successive came the chiefs of Lochlin's echoing woods. Tall as the stag of Morven, moved stately before them the king. His shining shield is on his side, like a flame on the heath at night; when the world is silent and dark, and the traveller sees some ghost sporting in the beam! Dimly gleam the hills around, and show indistinctly their oaks! A blast from the troubled ocean removed the settled mist. The sons of Erin appear, like a ridge of rocks on the coast; when mariners, on shores unknown, are trembling at veering winds!"

"As a hundred winds on Morven; as the streams of a hundred hills; as clouds fly successive over heaven; as the dark ocean assails the shore of the desert; so roaring, so vast, so terrible, the armies mixed on Lena's echoing heath. The groan of the people spread over the hills: it was like the thunder of night, when the clouds burst on Cona; and a thousand ghosts shriek at once on the hollow wind. Fingal rushed on in his strength, terrible as the spirit of Trenmor; when, in a whirlwind, he comes to Morven, to see the children of his pride. The oaks resound on their mountains, and the rocks fall down before him. Dimly seen, as lightens the night, he strides largely from hill to hill. Bloody was the hand of my father, when he whirled the gleam of his sword. He remembers the battles of his youth. The field is wasted in his course!

"Ryno went on like a pillar of fire. Dark is the brow of Gaul. Fergus rushed forward with feet of wind. Fillan, like the mist of the hill.

Ossian, like a rock, came down. I exulted in
the strength of the king. Many were the deaths
of my arm! dismal the gleam of my sword! My
locks were not then so grey; nor trembled my
hands with age. My eyes were not closed in
darkness; my feet failed not in the race!

"Who can relate the deaths of the people?
Who the deeds of mighty heroes? When Fingal,
burning in his wrath, consumed the sons of
Lochlin; groans swelled on groans from hill to
hill, till night had covered all."

"Such were our words, when Gaul's loud voice
came growing on the wind. He waved on high
the sword of his father. We rushed to death
and wounds. As waves, white-bubbling over
the deep, come swelling, roaring on; as rocks of
ooze meet roaring waves; so foes attacked and
fought. Man met with man, and steel with
steel. Shields sound, and warriors fall. As a
hundred hammers on the red son of the furnace,
so rose, so rung their swords!

"Gaul rushed on, like a whirlwind in Ardven.
The destruction of heroes is on his sword.
Swaran was like the fire of the desert in the
echoing heath of Gormal! How can I give to
the song the death of many spears? My sword
rose high, and flamed in the strife of blood.
Oscar, terrible wert thou, my best, my greatest
son! I rejoiced in my secret soul, when his
sword flamed over the slain. They fled amain
through Lena's heath. We pursued and slew.
As stones that bound from rock to rock; as axes
in echoing woods; as thunder rolls from hill to
hill, in dismal broken peals; so blow succeeded
to blow, and death to death, from the hand of
Oscar and mine."

The Songs of Selma, one of the fragments appended to the epic, attracted a great share of admiration. It is by this poem that Goethe portrayed one of the moods of his *Werther*, in whose heart, as he said, " Ossian had banished Homer ".

"Star of descending night! fair is thy light in the west! thou liftest thy unshorn head from thy cloud : thy steps are stately on thy hill. What dost thou behold in the plain? The stormy winds are laid. The murmur of the torrent comes from afar. Roaring waves climb the distant rock. The flies of evening are on their feeble wings ; the hum of their course is on the field. What dost thou behold, fair light? But thou dost smile and depart. The waves come with joy around thee : they bathe thy lovely hair. Farewell, thou silent beam! Let the light of Ossian's soul arise !

" And it does arise in its strength ! I behold my departed friends. Their gathering is on Lora, as in the days of other years. Fingal comes like a watery column of mist ; his heroes are around : And see the bards of song, grey-haired Ullin ! stately Ryno ! Alpin, with the tuneful voice ! the soft complaint of Minona ! How are ye changed, my friends, since the days of Selma's feast ? When we contended, like gales of spring, as they fly along the hill, and bend by turns the feebly-whistling grass.

" Minona came forth in her beauty ; with down-cast look and tearful eye. Her hair flew slowly on the blast, that rushed unfrequent from

the hill. The souls of the heroes were sad when
she raised the tuneful voice. Often had they
seen the grave of Salgar, the dark dwelling of
white-bosomed Colma. Colma left alone on the
hill, with all her voice of song! Salgar promised
to come: but the night descended around.
Hear the voice of Colma, when she sat alone on
the hill!

" COLMA.

"It is night; I am alone, forlorn on the hill
of storms. The wind is heard in the mountain.
The torrent pours down the rock. No hut
receives me from the rain; forlorn on the hill of
winds!

"Rise, moon! from behind thy clouds. Stars
of the night, arise! Lead me, some light, to the
place, where my love rests from the chase alone!
his bow near him, unstrung: his dogs panting
around him. But here I must sit alone, by the
rock of the mossy stream. The stream and the
wind roar aloud. I hear not the voice of my
love! Why delays my Salgar, why the chief of
the hill, his promise? Here is the rock, and
here the tree! here is the roaring stream! Thou
didst promise with night to be here. Ah!
whither is my Salgar gone? With thee I would
fly, from my father; with thee, from my brother
of pride. Our race have long been foes; we are
not foes, O Salgar!

"I sit in my grief! I wait for morning in my
tears! Rear the tomb, ye friends of the dead.
Close it not till Colma come. My life flies away
like a dream: why should I stay behind? Here
shall I rest with my friends, by the stream of the
sounding rock. When night comes on the hill;

when the loud winds arise ; my ghost shall stand in the blast, and mourn the death of my friends. The hunter shall hear from his booth. He shall fear but love my voice! For sweet shall my voice be for my friends : pleasant were her friends to Colma ! "

Another fragment, *Calthon and Colmal*, opens thus :—

" Pleasant is the voice of thy song, thou lonely dweller of the rock ! It comes on the sound of the stream, along the narrow vale. My soul awakes, O stranger ! in the midst of my hall. I stretch my hand to the spear, as in the days of other years. I stretch my hand, but it is feeble ; and the sigh of my bosom grows. Wilt thou not listen, son of the rock ! to the song of Ossian ? My soul is full of other times ; the joy of my youth returns. Thus the sun appears in the west, after the steps of his brightness have moved behind a storm : the green hills lift their dewy heads ; the blue streams rejoice in the vale. The aged hero comes forth on his staff ; his grey hair glitters in the beam. Dost thou not behold, son of the rock ! a shield in Ossian's hall ? It is marked with the strokes of battle ; and the brightness of its bosses has failed. That shield the great Dunthalmo bore, the chief of streamy Teutha. Dunthalmo bore it in battle, before he fell by Ossian's spear. Listen, son of the rock ! to the tale of other years ! "

The next passage is from *The War of Caros* :—

" A thousand spears arose around ; the people

of Caros rose. Why, daughter of Toscar, why that tear? My son, though alone, is brave. Oscar is like a beam of the sky; he turns around, and the people fall. His hand is the arm of a ghost, when he stretches it from a cloud; the rest of his thin form is unseen; but the people die in the vale! My son beheld the approach of the foe; he stood in the silent darkness of his strength. 'Am I alone,' said Oscar, 'in the midst of a thousand foes? Many a spear is there! many a darkly-rolling eye! Shall I fly to Ardven? But did my fathers ever fly? The mark of their arm is in a thousand battles. Oscar too shall be renowned! Come, ye dim ghosts of my fathers, and behold my deeds in war! I may fall; but I will be renowned like the race of the echoing Morven.' He stood, growing in his place, like a flood in a narrow vale! The battle came, but they fell: bloody was the sword of Oscar!

"The noise reached his people at Crona; they came like a hundred streams. The warriors of Caros fled; Oscar remained like a rock left by the ebbing sea. Now dark and deep, with all his steeds, Caros rolled his might along: the little streams are lost in his course; the earth is rocking round. Battle spreads from wing to wing: ten thousand swords gleam at once in the sky. But why should Ossian sing of battles? For never more shall my steel shine in war. I remember the days of my youth with grief; when I feel the weakness of my arm. Happy are they who fell in their youth, in the midst of their renown! They have not beheld the tombs of their friend; or failed to bend the bow of their strength. Happy art thou, O Oscar, in the midst of thy rushing blast. Thou often goest to the fields of thy fame, where Caros fled from thy lifted sword.

"Darkness comes on my soul, O fair daughter of Toscar! I behold not the form of my son at Carun; nor the figure of Oscar on Crona. The rustling winds have carried him far away; and the heart of his father is sad. But lead me, O Malvina! to the sound of my woods; to the roar of my mountain streams. Let the chase be heard on Cona; let me think on the days of other years. And bring me the harp, O maid! that I may touch it, when the light of my soul shall arise. Be thou near, to learn the song; future times shall hear of me! The sons of the feeble hereafter will lift the voice on Cona; and, looking up to the rocks, say, 'Here Ossian dwelt'. They shall admire the chiefs of old, the race that are no more! while we ride on our clouds, Malvina! on the wings of the roaring winds. Our voices shall be heard, at times, in the desert; we shall sing on the breeze of the rock."

Carthon is one of the best of the smaller poems. It contains the well-known " Desolation of Balclutha," which has often been set to music.

"A tale of the times of old! The deeds of days of other years'!

"The murmur of thy streams, O Lora! brings back the memory of the past. The sound of thy woods, Garmallar, is lovely in mine ear. Dost thou not behold, Malvina, a rock with its head of heath? Three aged pines bend from its face;

green is the narrow plain at its feet; there the flower of the mountain grows, and shakes its white head in the breeze. The thistle is there alone, shedding its aged beard. Two stones, half sunk in the ground, show their heads of moss. The deer of the mountain avoids the place, for he beholds a dim ghost standing there. The mighty lie, O Malvina! in the narrow plain of the rock.

"A tale of the times of old! The deeds of days of other years!

"Who comes from the land of strangers, with his thousands around him? the sunbeam pours its bright stream before him; his hair meets the wind of his hills. His face is settled from war. He is calm as the evening beam that looks, from the cloud of the west, on Cona's silent vale. Who is it but Comhal's son, the king of mighty deeds! He beholds his hills with joy, he bids a thousand voices rise. 'Ye have fled over your fields, ye sons of the distant land! The king of the world sits in his hall, and hears of his people's flight. He lifts his red eye of pride; he takes his father's sword. Ye have fled over your fields, sons of the distant land!'"

"Raise, ye bards, said the mighty Fingal, the praise of unhappy Moina. Call her ghost, with your songs, to our hills; that she may rest with the fair of Morven, the sunbeams of other days, the delight of heroes of old. I have seen the walls of Balclutha, but they were desolate. The fire had resounded in the halls: and the voice of the people is heard no more. The stream of Clutha was removed from its place, by the fall of the walls. The thistle shook, there, its lonely head : the moss whistled to the wind. The fox looked out from the windows, the rank grass of the wall waved round its head. Desolate is the dwelling of Moina, silence is in the house of her fathers. Raise the song of mourning, O bards ! over the land of strangers. They have but fallen before us : for, one day, we must fall. Why dost thou build the hall, son of the winged days ? Thou lookest from thy towers to-day ; yet a few years, and the blast of the desert comes ; it howls in thy empty court, and whistles round thy half-worn shield. And let the blast of the desert come ! we shall be renowned in our day ! The mark of my arm shall be in battle ; my name in the song of bards. Raise the song ; send round the shell : let joy be heard in my hall. When thou, sun of heaven, shall fail ! if thou shalt fail, thou mighty light ! if thy brightness is for a season, like Fingal ; our fame shall survive thy beams !

" Such was the song of Fingal, in the day of his joy. His thousand bards leaned forward from their seats, to hear the voice of the king. It was like the music of harps on the gale of the spring. Lovely were thy thoughts, O Fingal ! why had not Ossian the strength of thy soul ? But thou standest alone, my father ! who can equal the king of Selma ? "

The work was received with great praise. By January, 1762, Ossian was the talk of the town ; his only rival in popular interest was the Cock Lane ghost. Foremost in giving Macpherson a welcome was *The Critical Review*, then under

Smollett's influence, - and conspicuous as the Tory organ of literary opinion. The number for December, 1761, contained the first part of a notice extravagantly favourable, in which *Fingal* was strongly recommended to the public as a perfect work of its kind, answering to and fulfilling all the intention of epic poetry. It was praised in a more discriminate fashion in the *Annual Register;* [1] and the tone of the article leads us to attribute the criticism to Burke himself. The writer declared that the venerable author and his elegant translator had conferred immortality on each other; he described the poems as "these inestimable relicks of the genuine spirit of poetry, recovered from the obscurity of barbarism, the rust of fifteen hundred years, and the last breath of a dying language". There were many other reviews in a similar strain, and the work was generally admired; but mingled with the admiration was no small astonishment at the gentle manners and extraordinary generosity which the poems disclosed. The common opinion of the drawing-rooms was doubtless expressed by Boswell, who spoke of Ossian with enthusiasm, and preferred

[1] 1761, ii. 276.

him to Homer, Virgil and Milton. "*Fin-gal*," he wrote to Erskine, "shall accompany me. Take my word for it, he will make you feel you have a soul."[1]

But among the men of letters, while some were disposed to believe in the general authenticity of the poems, there was no lack of adverse criticism. Walpole, who changed his opinion half a dozen times, now declared that *Fingal* tired him, and that he would never believe that an ep c| in six books could be preserved amongst savages; the thing was plainly impossible.[2] In a letter written from Aberdeen, Beattie spoke cf "the universal deluge of approbation" poured upon the work both in London and in Scotland. But he pointed out, as an obvious fact, that the poems never existed previously in the form in which Macpherson published them; and that they were not of an epic but of a lyric cast. He expressed his belief that they would not live, as they showed "no know-

[1] See Boswell's correspondence with Erskine, letters of 17th December, 1761, and 10th January, 1762. On 22nd January, he tells Erskine that "*Fingal* has been warmly received in London. A second edition of it is just now come out."

[2] *Letters, ibid.*

ledge of the human heart"; and that what could
be said of Homer, that he was as much admired
three months as three thousand years ago,
would never be said of Ossian.[1] Gray, whose
earlier doubts seem to have been removed, read
Fingal with interest. "The epic poem," he
wrote,[2] "is foolishly so called; yet there is a
sort of plan and unity in it very strange for a
barbarous age; what I more admire are some
of the detached pieces."

In his preface and introductory dissertation
Macpherson refrained from clearly explaining
to the public that his epic had, as his literary
friends very well knew, been formed out of fragments; nay, in one passage, he spoke of laying
the work before his readers as he had found it.
But it is obvious that he did not thereby mean
his readers to believe that he had found it
entire; for in thanking the gentlemen in the
Highlands and Isles who had generously given
him all the assistance in their power, he stated
that it was by their means that he was enabled
to complete the epic poem which he presented

[1] Forbes' *Life of Beattie.*   Letter to Arbuthnot, 29th
March, 1762.

[2] Mason, *loc. cit.*

to the public. He declared that he had undertaken the journey in search of the poetical
remains of the old bards more from a desire
to comply with the request of several persons
of rank and taste, than from any hope of being
able to answer their expectations ; but when
he considered how much these ancient compositions had been neglected in the north of
Scotland, he had not, he thought, been unsuc-
cessful.

Up to the moment when he brought out
Fingal, there was, as far as we can judge, nothing
suspicious, certainly nothing arrogant or defiant,
in the temper in which Macpherson approached
the public. We know the impression which he
had produced upon his friends in private life.
Some of them were repelled by his air of shy
constraint, although it was not inexplicable in a
youth of poor origin and great ambition who
suddenly found himself an object of interest to
the very men with whom he aspired to be
numbered. Others, like Hume and Ramsay,
from what they had seen of him hitherto, praised
his modesty and good sense. If we remember
that the authenticity of his work had been freely
questioned for a year before he published it,

there is something commendable in the tone and
manner in which he met his critics.

" Poetry, like virtue, receives its reward after
death.   The fame which men pursued in vain
when living, is often bestowed upon them when
they are not sensible of it.   This neglect of living
authors is not altogether to be attributed to that
reluctance which men show in praising and re-
warding genius.   It often happens that the
man who writes differs greatly from the same
man in common life.   His foibles, however, are
obliterated by death ; and his better part, his
writings, remain: his character is formed from
them, and he that was no extraordinary man in
his own time, becomes the wonder of succeeding
ages.   From this source proceeds our veneration
for the dead : their virtues remain, but the
vices which were once blended with their virtues
have died with themselves.
    "This consideration might induce a man
diffident of his abilities to ascribe his own compositions to a person whose remote antiquity,
and whose situation, when alive, might well
answer for faults which would be inexcusable in
a writer of this age.   An ingenious gentleman
made the observation before he knew anything
but the name of the epic poem which is printed
in the following collection.   When he had read
it, his sentiments were changed.   He found it
abounded too much with those ideas that only
belong to the most early state of society, to be
the work of a modern poet; of this, I am persuaded, the public will be as thoroughly convinced as this gentleman was, when they shall
see the poems ; and that some will think not-

withstanding the disadvantages with which the works ascribed to Ossian appear, it would be a very uncommon instance of self-denial in me to disown them, were they really of my composition."

It will be objected that Macpherson's own observations are no evidence of his honesty. Those who · see falsehood in everything that came from his pen may, of course, believe what they please. It is inevitable that the bearing of any particular statement should depend upon the temper in which we approach it ; and the most that we can do is to try to adjust our temper to the general weight and effect of all the evidence known to us. By the light of the evidence known to them, many of Macpherson's contemporaries thought him a mere impostor. The reader may judge for himself. If he has followed the narrative thus far, he is in possession of facts unknown to Macpherson's contemporaries, and of information regarding the nature of Highland poetry unknown to Macpherson himself. But the passage from his preface is quoted mainly to show that when, as at first, civil language was used in throwing doubt upon the authenticity of his work, Macpherson, who was then unspoilt, could reply in terms that were certainly moderate and entirely free from arrogance.

At this time it was only to the Irish that he was contemptuous : and as there is not the slightest reason to believe that he obtained any of his materials from Ireland, his contempt for the Irish accusation of plagiarism was sufficiently just. An example of this charge is afforded by *Fingal Reclaimed,* a diatribe in which about this time an anonymous writer essayed to prove the theft. By others it was freely affirmed that the historical details of the royal families of Ireland and Morven were too circumstantial to be derived from bards and senachies ; but, as Ramsay points out, Macpherson's accounts were modest compared with those of the Irish writers ; and both of them drew their information from metrical histories.[1] The nature of the more discerning Irish criticism is well shown in a contemporary pamphlet by Ferdinando Warner, rector of Barnes in Surrey, a celebrated preacher of the day and a voluminous writer.[2] His pamphlet, entitled

[1] *Op. cit.*

[2] His *History of Ireland* shows some antiquarian research. For an account of him, see Nicholls' *Literary Anecdotes*, ii. 415.

Remarks on the History of Fingal, took the form
of "a letter to the Right Hon. Lord L——,"
probably Lord Lyttelton, dated Barnes, 2nd
February, 1762, in which he stated that in his
opinion the whole of the poems were probably the
work of an old Irish bard; and that, although
he admitted their beauty, and, in general, their
authenticity, he disputed all that Macpherson
said in his notes as to their historical aspect.
With a flourish of trumpets, modern critics
have proclaimed that Macpherson betrayed the
artificial construction of his epic by bringing
Cuchullin, who, according to tradition, lived in
the first century, into relation with Fingal,
who, according to similar tradition, lived in
the third; and this, although Macpherson did
not deny that the poem was collected from
fragments, and put together by himself, and
although he owned that the account which he
gave was different from that given by Irish
historians. In a modest way, Dr. Ferdinando
Warner made the same criticism; and he
deserves to be mentioned because, while he
was the earliest to show that Macpherson
combined legends that are said to belong to
different epochs, he perceived that the com-

bination did not affect the general authenticity
of the work.[1]   It is more than probable that
Macpherson found them already combined in
Scotch tradition.

Macpherson had, as we have seen, already
exhibited whatever originals he had to his friends
in Edinburgh ; he had published a proposal for
printing them, and, through lack of support, the
proposal had fallen to the ground. Whatever
these originals were,—whether they were the
old manuscripts which he had discovered, or
the transcripts which he and his friends had
made from oral recitation, he now, it seems,
placed them in the hands of his publishers in
London, where any one might have seen them
for the asking. His publishers advertised the
fact, and repeated the proposal for printing
them. As very few persons in London were
acquainted with Gaelic, few came to inspect
them ; and there were still fewer who were ready
to subscribe for the pleasure of putting them
into print. After lying for some months in the

---

[1] The same criticism was made, but in a form adverse to
the authenticity of the work, in 1772, by O'Halloran, in his
*Introduction to the Study of the History and Antiquities of
Ireland.*

publishers' shop in the Strand, the manuscripts were returned to their owner.[1] It is often asserted, by those who have not been at pains to examine the facts, that at no time was Macpherson either willing or able to produce the originals of his work ; but the assertion is manifestly inaccurate.

[1] See the publishers' letter, given on p. 249; and for further confirmation, Blair's statement to Henry Mackenzie, *Rep.*, App., p. 60.

CHAPTER IX.

The Charge of .Forgery. — Contemporary Hatred of the Scotch.—The "North Briton".—Churchill.—Blair's "Dissertation".—Publication of "Temora".—Johnson's Attitude. — Cesarotti. — Change in Macpherson's Conduct. — Boswell.— Hume's Letters to Blair.—Direct Testimony from the Highlands—its Result.

It is a far cry from a free or even a pretentious treatment of authentic materials to sheer imposture; and if allowance is made for the canons of criticism accepted in the eighteenth century, it will hardly be said that in giving an artistic form to his materials Macpherson was committing any very heinous crime. In the way in which he afterwards defended the authenticity of his work when it was impugned with astonishing vehemence, he made grave mistakes; but his error was in some measure due to the virulence of the attack. That the poems never previously existed in the form and shape in which he gave them to the world was proclaimed as though the fact took away all credit from the translator, and as though in his preface and dissertation he expressly denied the composite character of his work. A plagiarist must be uncommonly candid who quotes the source of his inspiration at the foot of his page; and Macpherson has never been accused of excessive candour. Nevertheless, his attempt to illustrate the text of his work by quoting passages from well-known authors—perhaps also his honesty in showing whence he obtained some of the niceties of his translation—was turned against him, and he was directly accused of the most brazen forgery.

Although for the success of his venture Macpherson had to some extent depended on the attention which had recently been drawn to the Highlands, he was in the same respect peculiarly unfortunate; for he soon found his work not only assailed with all the recognised weapons of criticism but also maliciously resented as a piece of Scotch impertinence. There can be no doubt that the bitterness with which it was attacked was due to the fierce hatred of the Scotch which then prevailed in London.

For centuries Scotchmen had been regarded as foreigners, and nothing that had occurred

since the Union had made them popular.
In political life they formed a compact and
isolated body, subject to ignominious disabilities and peculiarly liable to corruption.
The rising had put the seal to this national
hatred ; and thereafter if a writer hailed
from north of the Tweed, the fact was a
passport to abuse. Hume himself, who had
seen the first volume of his *History* attacked
with extraordinary rancour by all parties alike,
was so much disgusted by this rage against
his countrymen, that he more than once resolved never to set foot again on English
ground, nor have anything further to do with
what he contemptuously called "the barbarians
who inhabit the banks of the Thames". Garrick
was afraid to play Macbeth in tartan and kilt
for fear of thereby damning the piece ;[1] and
in Macklin's *Man of the World* the ridicule
of the Scotch in the person of Sir Pertinax
MacSycophant was received with the wildest
applause. If for many years before and after
Macpherson's productions appeared, it was
commonly held that no good thing could
come out of Scotland, it is clear that with

[1] See Doran's *Jacobite London,* ii. 350.

whatever interest they were awaited, they had little chance of fair treatment.

No Scotch work could have appeared at a more unfavourable opportunity than was offered by the close of the year 1761. In October the government of Pitt, who, by a combination of splendid abilities, had raised the fame and prosperity of the country to a height surpassed at no previous period of its history, was succeeded by a Tory reaction, with Bute, a Scotchman and a Jacobite, as the young King's favourite and chief Minister. The Court was crowded with his countrymen, most of them needy adventurers and eager place-hunters, at once audacious, subservient, and notoriously corrupt. The change provoked a storm of indignation which pervaded every class outside the Court. Bute himself attained a degree of unpopularity such as has seldom fallen to the lot of any English Minister; he was subjected to every kind of insult; he was burnt in effigy, attacked in the streets, and at last compelled, in fear of his life, to hire a gang of butchers and prizefighters to protect him.

The literature of the day was deeply infected with the venom of this enmity; and for a glimpse of it we have only to turn to the savage onslaught of Churchill, or to the notorious libels of the *North Briton.* Macpherson was known to be a friend and dependent of Bute, and his Ossian supplied an obvious butt for national ridicule. Wilkes had his fling at the Scotch in *The Poetry Professor,* a tirade in verse affixed to the number of the *North Briton* for 27th November, 1762. He bade the poets of the day keep their hands off the ancient writers :—

> " Oh forbear
> To spoil with sacrilegious hand
> The glories of the classic land.
> . . . Better be native in thy verse—
> What is *Fingal* but genuine Erse ?
> Which, all sublime, sonorous flows
> Like Hervey's *Thoughts* in drunken Prose."

> " When England's genius droops her wing
> So shall thy soil new wealth disclose ;
> So thy own *Thistle* choak the *Rose.*
> . . . Macpherson leads the flaming van,
> Laird of the New Fingalian clan."

Churchill's mockery in his *Prophecy of Eamine* was in the same strain :—

> " Thence issued forth, at great Macpherson's call,
> That old, new epic pastoral, *Fingal.*
> .   .   .   .

Now be the muse disrobed of all her pride,
Be all the glare of verse by truth supplied,
And if plain nature pours a simple strain,
Which Bute may praise and Ossian not disdain,
Ossian, sublimest, simplest bard of all
Whom English infidels Macpherson call,
Then round my head shall Honour's ensigns
    wave,
And pensions mark me for a willing slave."

And in *The Ghost*, after an ignoble attack on
Johnson, he has his laugh at the critics :—

  "By truth inspired, our critics go
    To track *Fingal* in Highland snow,
    To form their own and others' creed
    From manuscripts they cannot read ".

While the poems met with a mixed reception
in London, Macpherson's friends in Edinburgh
were still busy singing their praises. Blair, who
was professor of Rhetoric and Belles Lettres,
had made them the subject of some elaborate
lectures. He took them in all good faith as
the genuine work of a bard in the third century,
discoursed on the character of their antiquity
and their poetical spirit, and, to use his own
words, "after applying the rules of criticism to
Fingal as an epic poem," he proceeded " to
examine the merit of Ossian's compositions in

general, with regard to description, imagery and sentiment ". This was putting the work to a strain which it was unable to bear ; but such mistaken zeal made it all the easier for Macpherson to persevere in an idea which, as we have seen, was probably first suggested to him by the distinguished professor. If Blair, instead of waxing enthusiastic over the fancied discovery of a national epic, had applied to an examination of the poems, not any formal rules of criticism, but a little poetic genius, with an admixture of common-sense, he could never· have given Macpherson any ground for supposing that the collection of lyrical pieces which he produced was characterised by any real unity, or possessed any other mark of a true epic. It was only with the prevailing ignorance of the nature of the poetry of the Highlands, an ignorance shared by Macpherson himself, that he could seriously discuss the poems as though they were a genuine legacy from the third century. But the lectures appealed to his hearers, and by their desire they were enlarged and given to the public as a *Critical Dissertation on the Poems of Ossian.* Blair's work was published in London at the beginning of the year 1763, and the reviews praised it as a masterly piece of criticism.

Macpherson was encouraged to proceed; and in March, 1763, he brought out the second instalment of his work. This appears to have been undertaken at Bute's suggestion, to whom it was openly dedicated; and it is said that the expenses of its publication came out of that nobleman's pocket. It was entitled *Temora, an Ancient Epic Poem, in eight books, together with several other Poems, composed by Ossian the son of Fingal, translated from the Galic language.* To this he prefixed a separate dissertation, in which he explained that he had collected the materials for it on his journey in the Highlands and Isles, and by the assistance of correspondents since he left the country; and that the story of the poem, with which he had long been acquainted, enabled him to reduce the broken members of the piece into the order in which they now appeared. For the ease of the reader he had divided it into books, as he had previously done with the poem of *Fingal;* and the title of Epic was also imposed upon it by himself. For the satisfaction of those who doubted the authenticity of this and the former work, he appended a specimen of the original, and for that purpose fixed upon the seventh book. To print any part of the former work was, he added, unnecessary, as a copy of the originals had lain for many months in the booksellers' hands for the inspection of the curious.

The specimen which he now published was afterwards carefully examined by the Highland Society, and in the opinion of their committee it contained some imperfections and modernisms. Macpherson himself, in publishing it, apologised for its uncouth appearance, and stated that he had, in fact, departed from the orthography of the bards. To those who remember the nature of the assistance which Macpherson received from his friends in Badenoch on returning from his journey, the character of this original will not be very doubtful.

It will be clear to any one reading Macpherson's second dissertation with care that it displays him in a much more courageous attitude towards his materials than he had ventured to assume in the previous production. In the quasi-historical part of it he laid down as undoubted facts matters that were in high dispute ; and he went out of his way to attack the Irish historians, Keating and O'Flaherty, as idle fabulists, whose veracity was as doubt-ful as their ability. He claimed that *Temora* was infinitely more valuable than *Fingal* for the light it threw on the history of the times. Further, he spoke of the suspicions engendered by the former work as beneath his notice, and as giving him no concern, since he always had it in his power to remove them. The inference from the tone which Macpherson here adopted is sufficiently obvious ; and from an examina-tion of *Temora* itself, it is impossible to resist the conclusion that on whatever authentic materials it may have been based, Macpherson dealt with them in this work in a much freer fashion, and with many more interpolations of his own than he had made in the case of *Fingal;* and while it is by no means devoid of much true poetical feeling and imagery, there is a marked increase of the tendency to sheer bombast. Although the work was widely read, and praised in the few reviews that were friendly to the Scotch, the literary circles of London received it with open ridicule.

Johnson was at this time, in the name given

him by Smollett, "the great Cham of Literature ".
It was some years since he had given his last
Rambler to the public, and completed the labours
of his *Dictionary;* and he was now securely established in the seat that had once been filled by
Dryden and by Pope. Although he had formerly
written of pensioners in terms of great disparage-
ment, he was now in receipt of a pension himself;
not, it was agreed, for anything that he was
expected to do, but for what he had already
done. With a circle of devoted friends about
him, and a faithful chronicler beginning to record
his sayings, he assumed, and exercised with
vigour, all the functions of a literary dictator ;
and whether his opinions were good or bad,
they carried weight.

From the beginning he had, as Boswell tells
us, not only denied the authenticity of the poems,
but, what was still more annoying to their admirers, he refused to admit that they had any
merit at all. He freely expressed the opinion
that the work was unmitigated rubbish. When
Blair asked him whether he thought that any
man of a modern age could have written such
poems, he replied : " Yes, sir ; many men, many
women, and many children ;" and to Reynolds

he afterwards declared that "a man might write such stuff for ever, if he would abandon his mind to it". To discover the explanation of Johnson's contempt for the poems is in nowise a difficult task; nor, in spite of the efforts of certain eminent critics, is it at all necessary to go very far for it. Macaulay, for instance, in approving Johnson's opinion, took it upon himself to suspect that he despised the poems because they had a superficial air of originality. A writer [1] of our own day has observed that since the poems formed one of the earliest and most remarkable manifestations of that growing taste for "Nature," as opposed to civilisation, which found its strongest expression in Rousseau, it was inevitable that Johnson should regard them with scorn. It is beyond question that the poems appealed to an interest, then becoming general, in the conditions of antique or even of savage life; but the feeling for nature displayed in Macpherson's productions has nothing to do with any attack upon the order of society; and if the Ossianic poems are

[1] Mr. Leslie Stephen, in his *Johnson* (" English Men of Letters "). M. Taine, it seems, took a similar view; see his *Hist. of Eng. Lit.*, ii. 220, ed. of 1892.

to be drawn under the ban which proscribes the doctrines of Rousseau, it is hardly possible for the Homeric poems, or the *Nibelungenlied*, to escape a similar fate. The idyllic peace which Rousseau imagined to be a feature of primitive life in a wholly ideal "state of Nature" would be rudely disturbed by the joy of battle and the glory of conquest which animate Fingal's heroes, and the gaiety of his untutored savage scarcely accords with the passionate melancholy of Ossian's song.

The explanation of Johnson's contempt may be found in causes much less subtle and remote. In simple language the poems were not of the literature for which he was ever likely to have any approbation. With all his great gifts and his admirable sagacity, his tastes were notoriously narrow; and the contempt which he felt for Macpherson would probably have been bestowed in equal measure on a Shelley or a Keats. He despised the poems because he had no interest in their antiquity, and no feeling for the peculiar quality of their beauty; and as their beauty was exciting the admiration of some of his friends, he burst out into a torrent of abuse. The range of his literary sympathies was the range of the literary conventions that had prevailed in his youth; and if there were nothing else to show that he was firmly fixed within these limits it would be evident from the fact that he preferred Pope's version of the *Iliad* to the original. For the best writers of his own time he had little or no praise; and when he ventured on any praise, it was often misplaced. He had, for instance, some admiration for Richardson, but none for Fielding; he put Goldsmith in the first class of historians, and above Hume or Robertson; he had no doubt of the success of Hoole's *Cleonice*, a forgotten work by a forgotten writer. Gray he called a dull fellow and a mechanical poet, and his works mere cucumbers raised in a hot-bed; he commended Young's *Night Thoughts,* and spoke with faint approval of Thomson's *Castle of Indolence;* but he could see nothing in *Gulliver's Travels,* or in *Tristram Shandy.* His sympathies were bound up with London, and the life and interests of London; if he turned to the past, he found the Athenians a people of brutes, and mere barbarians; if he turned to the present, the French were not only silly but unmannered; and Voltaire, one of the greatest men of letters of all time, was dismissed

as *vir acerrimi ingenii et paucarum literarum*.
Life in the country was a waste of existence;
the Grampians were a row of "considerable
protuberances," and the finest landscape paled
before the glories of Fleet Street and Charing
Cross. There was therefore nothing surprising
in his contempt for poems which derived half
their interest from an alleged antiquity, and half
their beauty from the reflection of the best
Highland scenery.

He had, it is true, some Scotch friends; but
he professed an extravagant hatred for Scotland
as a country and the Scotch as a nation; and
there can be no doubt that this was an element in the abuse which he poured upon Macpherson. And in connection with his opinion
that the poems were a Scotch forgery there
was an earlier experience which could not
be overlooked. Some thirteen years previously
one Lauder, also a Scotch schoolmaster, had
fabricated a mass of Latin poetry, partly taken
from Grotius and other modern Latin writers,
which he proclaimed as the archetype of *Paradise
Lost*. Among the elect whom he deceived
was Johnson himself, who had taken a great
interest in the work and supplied Lauder with

a preface and postscript. Johnson was not likely to forget the indignation which he had felt when the fraud was detected, or thereafter to look kindly on any other Scotch work of doubtful authenticity.

Finally, it does not appear that at the time when the poems were published, Johnson made the slightest effort to investigate the grounds on which they were pronounced authentic. He thought them a mere book of the hour, and paid them no serious attention. It is possible that he knew nothing of the announcement that the alleged originals were to be seen at Becket's shop; but in any case he took no notice of it. Some twelve years later, when the reputation of the poems seemed to be firmly established, he went out of his way to attack them; and the strength of his language led to a furious correspondence with Macpherson.

In spite of all the ridicule and attack to which they were subjected in London, the poems continued to grow in favour in this country, and they began to make their way abroad. They ultimately became very popular on the continent, where they soon appeared in various languages. About this time a reputa-

tion was made for them in Italy by the enthusiastic praise which they drew from the Abbé
Cesarotti.   Born at Padua in 1730, of an ancient
and noble family, Cesarotti had quickly won
fame as a scholar and a poet; and Macpherson
must have been flattered at receiving his compliments.   In a letter still preserved, Cesarotti
wrote to offer the congratulations of his
countrymen on the happy discovery of a new
world of poetry, and spoke of his intention to
translate the works of Ossian into his own
language; although, as he admitted, they had
encountered no small incredulity amongst educated Italians.[1]   The letter was forwarded by
the English consul at Venice, to whom Macpherson sent the following elegant reply :—

" London, 4th May, 1763.

" Sir,

      " Nothing could afford me more pleasure
than the Abbé Cesarotti's letter which you did
me the honour to transmit to me.   I happened,
unfortunately, to be absent from London when
your letter came, otherwise I would have had
sooner acknowledged the great obligation you
have laid upon me.   The elegance of sentiment
and the critical knowledge which the abbé
displays convince me sufficiently that he will do
great justice to Ossian's poems in the translation

[1] British Museum Addit. MSS. 22,899, f. 5.

he intends. I have ordered by the first ship to Venice two copies of a second volume of Ossian's compositions ;—one I intend for you, and the other for the abbé. The dissertation prefixed to this work will throw light on its antiquity ; but if that is not sufficient to satisfy the abbé concerning the authenticity, I will transmit to you such further light as he may require. I must repeat my thanks to you, Sir, for the valuable correspondence you have procured for me; for allow me to assure you that it will greatly add to my happiness to hear as frequently as is convenient from you and the Abbé Cesarotti.

" I have the honour to be, Sir,
" Your most obedient and most humble servant,

" JAMES MACPHERSON.

"N.B.—A letter will always find me at the British Coffee House, London." [1]

In the same month Dr. Stukeley, a well-known antiquary of the time, published *A Letter to Mr. Macpherson*, in which he drew a comparison, favourable to the authenticity of the poems, between the alleged Druidical relics on Salisbury Plain and the Ossianic lore.

Under the prosperity which he had now attained, Macpherson began to give himself airs. Up to the time when he published *Temora* his personal conduct had been without reproach,

[1] British Museum Addit. MSS. 22,889, f. 165.

and he had not shown himself unwilling to
satisfy his critics. But with some men effort
is more invigorating than success, and he had
succeeded beyond his wildest expectations. A
rancorous attack had been made upon him, and
it is hardly matter for surprise that a young
man of spirit and of undoubted genius should
have met it with disdain. But Macpherson went
further : he resolved henceforth to treat all
doubt as to the authenticity of his work, from
whatever quarter it came, with a sullen defiance.
His resolution was partly the outcome of mere
mettle, and partly of a less respectable quality.
He was six-and-twenty, and flattered to the top
of his bent. What happened with him was
only what happens with most literary adventurers whose success is immediate and greater
than their strict deserts ; he contracted the foolish temper in which a man regards all criticism
as ignorant or impertinent, and declines to take
advice from any one. He had made some £1200
by his work, and he was proud of his personal
achievements ; nay if we may trust certain indications contained in the prefaces to later editions,
he was secretly gratified that any one could suppose him the actual author of the whole of it.

He succumbed to one of the infirmities of the literary nature, and, instead of quietly preparing for other work, he began to advertise his genius. According to an account of him given by Boswell, he indulged in some desperate rodomontade in the coffee houses, and posed as a moral sceptic. That was the fashion of the hour. It can hardly be doubted that Boswell's life in London, and his intimacy with Wilkes, Churchill, Lloyd, and their companions, gave him ample opportunity of hearing the worst scandal about his countrymen; and it is sufficiently intelligible that in talking with Johnson he should have put the worst construction on what he heard.[1]

[1] Most readers of *Johnson's Life* will remember a passage in which Boswell speaks of " an impudent fellow from Scotland, who affected to be a savage, and railed at all established systems "; provoking from Johnson the following remarks : " There is nothing surprising in this, Sir. He wants to make himself conspicuous. He would tumble in a hogstye, as long as you looked at him, and called to him to come out. But let him alone, never mind him, and he'll soon give it over." When Boswell added that the same person maintained that there was no distinction between virtue and vice, " Why, Sir," said Johnson, " if the fellow does not think as he speaks, he is lying ; and I do not see what honour he can propose to himself from having the character of a liar. But if he does really think that there is no distinction between virtue and vice, why, Sir, when he leaves our houses, let us

But we have other and more trustworthy evidence of the change which now showed itself in Macpherson's behaviour.   Hume, who had hitherto expressed a general belief in the authenticity of the poems, had also been led to form a high opinion of his young friend's character ; and there can be no doubt that the philosopher had a fellow-feeling with his countryman in the way in which he had been assailed.   But now his opinion underwent a complete change; and as there was never a philosopher more indulgent or generous than Hume, he must have had good grounds for reversing his judgment.   He had suggested to Macpherson that it would be well to ask those who had given him materials in the Highlands for their direct testimony.   Macpherson, in a passion, refused to take any step that would look like a deference on his part to the attack upon his veracity.   Hume then made his appeal to Blair; and as his letter is in some ways remarkable, it may here be given almost entire.

count our spoons " (1763, æt. 54).   It does not appear that Johnson knew to whom his vigorous remarks applied ; but that it was Macpherson is shown by the volume of *Boswelliana* (p. 210), published by the Grampian Club.

" Lisle St., Leicester Fields, 19th Sept., 1763.

" Dear Sir,

" I live in a place where have I the pleasure
of frequently hearing justice done to your dissertation, but never heard it mentioned in a
company where some one person or other did
not express his doubts with regard to the
authenticity of the poems which are its subject,
and I often hear them totally rejected, with
disdain and indignation, as a palpable and most
impudent forgery. This opinion has indeed
become very prevalent among the men of letters
in London; and I can foresee, that in a few
years the poems, if they continue to stand on
their present footing, will be thrown aside, and
will fall into final oblivion. It is in vain to say
that their beauty will support them, independent
of their authenticity. No! that beauty is not so
much to the general taste as to ensure you of
this event; and if people be once disgusted with
the idea of a forgery, they are thence apt to
entertain a more disadvantageous notion of the
excellency of the production itself. The absurd
pride and caprice of Macpherson himself, who
scorns, as he pretends, to satisfy anybody that
doubts his veracity, has tended much to confirm
this general scepticism; and I must own, for
my own part, that though I have had many
particular reasons to believe these poems
genuine, more than it is possible for any English-
man of letters to have, yet I am not entirely
without my scruples on that head. You think
that the internal proofs in favour of the poems are
very convincing. So they are; but there are also
internal reasons against them, particularly from
the manners, notwithstanding all the art with

which you have endeavoured to throw a vernish on that circumstance; and the preservation of such long and such connected poems, by oral tradition alone, during a course of fourteen centuries, is so much out of the ordinary course of human affairs that it requires the strongest reasons to make us believe it. My present purpose therefore is, to apply to you, in the name of all the men of letters of this, and I may say of all other countries, to establish this capital point, and to give us proofs that these poems are, I do not say so antient as the age of Severus, but that they were not forged within these five years by James Macpherson. These proofs must not be arguments but testimonies: people's ears are fortified against the former; the latter may yet find their way, before the poems are consigned to total oblivion. Now, the testimonies may, in my opinion, be of two kinds. Macpherson pretends that there is an ancient manuscript of part of Fingal in the family, I think, of Clanranald. Get that fact ascertained by more than one person of credit; let these persons be acquainted with Gaelic; let them compare the original and the translation; and let them testify the fidelity of the latter.

" But the chief point in which it will be necessary for you to exert yourself will be, to get positive testimony from many different hands, that such poems are regularly recited in the Highlands, and have there long been the entertainment of the people. This testimony must be as particular as it is positive. It will not be sufficient that a Highland gentleman or clergyman says or writes to you that he has heard such poems; nobody questions that there are traditional poems in that part of the country, where the names of Ossian and Fingal, and Oscar and Gaul, are mentioned in every stanza. The only doubt is, whether these poems have any farther resemblance to the poems published by Macpherson. I was told by Bourke, a very ingenious Irish gentleman, the author of a tract on the Sublime and Beautiful, that on the first publication of Macpherson's book, all the Irish cried out : ' We know all these poems ; we have always heard them from our infancy ' ; but when he asked more particular questions, he could never learn that any one had ever heard or could repeat the original of any one paragraph of the pretended translation. This generality, then, must be carefully guarded against, as being of no authority.

" Your connections among your brethren of the clergy may here be of great use to you. You may easily learn the names of all ministers of that country who understand the language of it. You may write to them, expressing the doubts that have arisen, and desiring them to send for such of the bards as remain, and make them rehearse their ancient poems. Let the clergymen then have the translation in their hands, and let them write back to you, and inform you that they heard such a one (naming him), living in such a place, rehearse the original of such a passage, from such a page to such a page of the English translation, which appeared exact and faithful. If you give to the public a sufficient number of such testimonies, you may prevail. But I venture to foretell to you that nothing less will serve the purpose, nothing less will so much as command the attention of the public.

" Becket tells me that he is to give us a new edition of your *Dissertation*, accompanied with

some remarks on *Temora.* Here is a favourable
opportunity for you to execute this purpose. You
have a just and laudable zeal for the credit of
these poems. They are, if genuine, one of the
greatest curiosities, in all respects, that ever was
discovered in the commonwealth of letters ; and
the child is, in a manner, become yours by adop-
tion, as Macpherson has totally abandoned all
care of it. These motives call upon you to exert
yourself, and I think it were suitable to your
candour, and most satisfactory also to the reader,
to publish all the answers to all these letters you
write, even though some of these letters should
make somewhat against your own opinion in this
affair. We shall always be the more assured that
no arguments are strained beyond their proper
force, and no contrary arguments suppressed,
where such an entire communication is made to us.
Becket joins me heartily in this application ; and
he owns to me, that the believers in the authenticity of the poems diminish every day among
the men of sense and reflection. Nothing less
than what I propose can throw the balance on
the other side. I depart from hence in about
three weeks, and should be glad to hear your
resolution before that time. . . .

"I am,

" Yours sincerely,

" DAVID HUME." [1]

Blair took up the challenge at once.

" Edinburgh, 29th September, 1763.

" Dear Sir,

" I am much obliged to you for the information you have communicated to me, and for the

---

[1] Given in Malcolm Laing's *Hist. of Scotland,* iv. 496.

concern you show that justice should be done to our Highland poems. From what I saw myself when at London, I could easily believe that the disposition of men of letters was rather averse to their reception as genuine ; but I trusted that the internal character of their authenticity, together with the occasional testimonies given to them by Highland gentlemen, who are everywhere scattered, would gradually surmount those prejudices. For my own part, it is impossible for me to entertain the smallest doubt of their being real productions, and ancient ones too, of the Highlands. Neither Macpherson's parts, though good, nor his industry, were equal to such a forgery. The whole publication, you know, was in its first rise accidental. Macpherson was entreated and dragged into it. Some of the MSS. sent to him passed through my hands. Several of them he translated, in a manner, under my eye. He gave me these native and genuine accounts of them, which bore plain characters of truth. What he said was often confirmed to me by others. I had testimonies from several Highlanders concerning their authenticity, in words strong and explicit. And setting all this aside, is it a thing which any man of sense can suppose, that Macpherson would venture to forge such a body of poetry, and give it to the public as ancient poems and songs, well known at this day through all the Highlands of Scotland, when he could have been refuted and exposed by every one of his own countrymen ? Is it credible that he could bring so many thousand people into a conspiracy with him to keep his secret ? or that some would not be found who, attached to their own ancient songs, would not cry out : 'These are not the poems we deal in. You have forged characters

and sentiments we know nothing about; you have
modernised and dressed us up; we have much
better songs and poems of our own.' Who but
John Bull could entertain the belief of an
imposture so incredible as this? The utmost I
should think any rational scepticism could suppose is this, that Macpherson might have sometimes interpolated, or endeavoured to improve,
by some corrections of his own. Of this I am
verily persuaded there was very little, if any at
all. Had it prevailed, we would have been able
to trace more marks of inconsistency, and a
different hand and style; whereas these poems
are more remarkable for nothing than an entire,
and supported, and uniform consistency of character and manner through the whole.

"However, seeing we have to do with such
incredulous people, I think it were a pity not to
do justice to such valuable monuments of genius.
I have already, therefore, entered upon the task
you prescribe me, though I foresee it may give
some trouble. I have writ by last post to Sir
James Macdonald, who is fortunately at this time
in the Isle of Skye. I have also, through the
Laird of Macleod, writ to Clanranald, and likewise to two clergymen in the Isle of Skye, men of
letters and character; one of them, Macpherson,
minister of Sleat, the author of a very learned
work about to be published concerning the antiquities of Scotland. Several others in Argyleshire, the Islands, and other poetical regions,
worthy clergymen, who are well versed in the
Gaelic, I intend also without delay to make
application to.

"My requisition to them all is for such positive and express testimony as you desire; MSS.
if they have any, compared before witnesses with

the printed book, and recitations of bards compared in the same manner. . . .

"I am in some difficulty with Macpherson himself in this affair. Capricious as he is, I would not willingly hurt or disoblige him; and yet I apprehend that such an inquiry as this, which is like tracing him out, and supposing his veracity called in question, will not please him. I must write him by the next post, and endeavour to put the affair in such a light as to soften him; which you, if you see him, may do likewise, and show him the necessity of something of this kind being done; and with more propriety, perhaps, by another than by himself. . . .

"HUGH BLAIR."[1]

To this Hume sent the following reply :—

"6th October, 1763.

"I am very glad you have undertaken the task which I used the freedom to recommend to you. Nothing less than what you propose will serve the purpose. You need expect no assistance from Macpherson, who flew into a passion when I told him of the letter I had wrote to you. But you must not mind so strange and heteroclite a mortal, than whom I have scarce ever known a man more perverse and unamiable. He will probably depart for Florida with Governor Johnston, and I would advise him to travel among the Chickisaws or Cherokees, in order to train him and civilise him. . . .

"Since writing the above, I have been in company with Mrs. Montagu, a lady of great dis-

[1] MSS. Roy. Soc. of Edinburgh.

14

tinction in this place, and a zealous partisan of
Ossian. I told her of your intention, and even
used the freedom to read your letter to her.
She was extremely pleased with your project;
and the rather as the Duc de Nivernois, she
said, had talked to her much on that subject last
winter, and desired, if possible, to get collected
some proofs of the authenticity of these poems,
which he proposed to lay before the Académie
des Belles Lettres at Paris. You see, then, that
you are upon a great stage in this inquiry and
that many people have their eyes upon you. . . .

"Please to write to me as soon as you make
any advances, that I may have something to say
on the subject to the *literati* of Paris." . . .[1]

The information which Blair collected has
already been given in the account of Macpherson's doings in the Highlands, which is derived from the letters received in the course of
the inquiry. These letters were, some eighteen
months afterwards, printed in an Appendix to a
second edition of Blair's *Dissertation;* and for a
time they appear to have put the critics out of
countenance. On July 1, 1765, we find Blair
writing to Hume in triumph : "Have I not
silenced all infidelity and even scepticism concerning Fingal in the Appendix to my *Dissertation*? . . . Will you still have any scruples ?"[2]

[1] MSS. Roy. Soc. of Edinburgh.
[2] Laing's *Hist.*, iv. 500.

But Hume persisted in his scruples; and by an application of his well-known argument from probability, refused to admit any evidence, however positive, in support of a theory which he could not reconcile with common-sense.[1] This was the theory, to which Macpherson was unfortunately led to commit himself, that the poems had been handed down from the third century. But it was one thing to show that on the question of antiquity Macpherson was himself mistaken or was misleading the public; and another, to refute the evidence adduced by Blair that his work was drawn in the main from poetry actually recited in the Highlands.

[1] See his letter to Gibbon, March 18, 1776. Gibbon's *Misc. Works*, i. 225. Hume wrote an essay on the poems, which he condemned as tiresome and insipid; but, out of deference to the feelings of his friend Blair, it was not published. It may be found in Burton's *Life*, i., App., p. 471.

CHAPTER X.

VISITS NORTH AMERICA.—RETURNS TO WRITE FOR
THE · PRESS.—HIS "INTRODUCTION TO THE
HISTORY OF GREAT BRITAIN".—TRANSLATES
THE "ILIAD".—CONTINUES HUME'S "HIS-
TORY".—CARTE'S PAPERS.—VISITS PARIS.—
PUBLISHES THE "ORIGINAL PAPERS".—THE
ATTACK UPON THEM.

IN the story of Macpherson's life we now
approach a period which, although it was by no
means uneventful, was not marked by much
work of abiding importance ; nor is it much
illuminated by personal detail. A brief chapter
will suffice for it.

Hume had stated that his untamed young
friend would probably depart for Florida. By
the Treaty of Paris, Spain had, in February, 1763,
ceded that colony to England ; and in October,
one George Johnstone was gazetted Governor
of the Western Provinces and ordered to Pensecola. Like most of the other American
Governors, Johnstone was a Scotchman. Macpherson was offered an appointment as his
secretary, and in addition the posts of president

of the council and surveyor-general. It was a
strange shift in the breeze of his fortune ; and of
the reasons which led him to yield to it we have
no knowledge : he may have resented the treatment which he was receiving from men of letters
in London, or he may have found himself in
pecuniary or other difficulties. Certain it is that
in the early part of the following year he set his
sails for America. He was absent about two
years ; but only a portion of that time was spent
at Pensecola, for he soon quarrelled with his
chief, and departed on a visit to some of the
other provinces. After a tour in the West
Indies he returned in 1766.

As surveyor-general he had received a salary
of £200 a year. In a day when pensions
formed a larger part of the machinery of the
State than at present, Macpherson was allowed
to retain it for life, on the condition, so far as
can be gathered, that he should devote himself
henceforth to political writing.

This was no unattractive or unimportant
occupation, for it was at that time that the
press began to acquire its strong influence on
public opinion. In spite of prohibitive duties
and numerous prosecutions for libel, newspapers

had been steadily increasing in number during the previous twenty years; by the support or opposition which they offered to the Government, they had gradually become a political power, and their support was a matter of no small moment. Smollett tells us that a nobleman who had been a member of several administrations declared that one good writer was of more importance to the Government than twenty placemen in the House.[1] The principles of a paper were not then, as they are now, enunciated in anonymous leading articles; but they were clearly expressed in the selection of the news which the editors chose to publish, and more especially in the letters which they admitted. It was by attracting political letters of a controversial character that the newspapers began to absorb both the political periodical and the vast literature of pamphlets which, at an earlier date, formed the ordinary channel for the expression of educated popular opinion.[2] Most of the letters thus published appeared over assumed names; and they continued to increase in number and im-

[1] *Letter to Caleb Whiteford.*
[2] See Mr. Lecky's *History*, iii. 228-233.

portance until, in the early part of 1769, the letters of "Junius" attracted general attention.

Some of the best writers of the time were engaged in this kind of journalism. Smollett, for instance, wrote regularly in the paper called *The Briton*, until he was silenced by Wilkes with his *North Briton*. Macpherson was now engaged on behalf of the Government; and he owed his place, it is said, to the favour of Lord North, who in 1767 was Chancellor of the Exchequer and in 1770 Prime Minister. Whether he wrote much or little in this capacity, most of it is buried in obscurity; but we learn that, under the signatures of "Musæus" and "Scævola," he attempted a reply to the letters of "Junius".[1] He also appears to have written a variety of pamphlets, of which two only, written at a later date, and hereafter to be noticed in their due place, have been preserved. If we call to mind the sort of political language that was then tolerated, it is perhaps not to be regretted that we have little knowledge of Macpherson's contributions to the journalism of his day.

[1] Robert Chalmers, in the first edition of his *Cyclop. of English Literature*, i. 625, states that amongst Macpherson's

But his political employment did not interfere with the desire to continue his literary career. It was the age of historians, great and small, and the Scotch had not been the least conspicuous in that branch of literature. Hume and Robertson had already made a name for themselves; Gibbon was preparing for his work; and among a number of minor writers who were not called by nature to the office of historian, Smollett had produced his complete *History of England*, and Goldsmith his *History of Rome*, and of *England*. With these high and low examples before him, Macpherson also began to look to history as a subject for his elegant pen.

He took a continuous and increasing interest in the remains of Celtic antiquity, and about this time set himself to a laborious inquiry into the Celtic element in the early civilisation of these islands. Certainly the work was not without its interest, or, it may be said, without its importance; for Macpherson represented to his own generation the crude beginnings of the

posthumous papers he found drafts of their replies, with these and other signatures. If the reader is pleased to turn to the letters of Junius, he will find a retort to "Scævola" by "Philo Junius" in letter lx., 15th October, 1771.

study of Celtic archæology and literature. Although his speculations are rough, inaccurate, and devoid of any historical value, he deserves, perhaps, a somewhat better treatment than he has received at the hands of those who since his day have pursued that study in a scientific spirit and in the light of better knowledge. In 1771 he published the results of his inquiry as *An Introduction to the History of Great Britain and Ireland.* This, as the lengthy title of the work proceeded to announce, was an examination of the origin, religion, future state, character, manners, morality, amusements, persons, manner of life, houses, navigation, commerce, languages, government, kings, general assemblies, courts of justice, and juries of the Britons, Scots, Irish, and Anglo-Saxons. It was a mere glorification of the Celts, and its aim was to show, what Macpherson unquestioningly believed, that most of our early civilisation might be traced to their institutions. But he was well aware that he could not expect much sympathy either for his work or for the views which he was maintaining. "Inquiries into antiquity," he wrote in his preface, "are so unpopular that without any of the ordinary incitements to literary labours the author was induced to proceed by the sole motive of private amusement." Some of the materials for the volume were obtained from MS. notes left by his friend the minister of Sleat, who in 1768 had published his *Critical Dissertations* on the origin and antiquities of the Caledonians.

The work was bitterly attacked as a piece of Celtic impertinence. Pinkerton drew some attention to himself by a furious onslaught on the Celts *en masse*, whom he described as a horde of savages; and he abused Macpherson in the grossest fashion as a "frontless impostor".[1] " The empty vanity, shallow reading, vague assertion, and etymological nonsense in the productions are," he declared, " truly risible." Hume, however, though he did not agree with its con-

[1] Pinkerton's antipathy to anything Celtic amounted almost to a mania. Though Edward Llwyd had clearly pointed out an affinity between Celtic and other European languages, and although Sir William Jones afterwards brought reasons to show that Celtic had probably the same origin as Sanscrit, Pinkerton declared that "the real Celtic" was as remote from the Greek as the Hottentot from the language of the Lapps. Pinkerton's pretensions were quietly put down by Scott in his introduction to *The Minstrelsy of the Scottish Border*, appended to the edition of 1830. See Scott's *Poetical Works*, one vol., ed. 1866, p. 548.

clusions, found it to contain "a great deal of genius and good writing"; and he sent Macpherson a kindly message through a common friend, Colonel Dow, of the East India Company's service.[1] In the following year an attempt was made by John Whittaker to refute its statements, in a volume entitled *The Genuine History of the Britons Asserted;*[2] but, nevertheless, Macpherson's work reached a second and even a third edition. It may be mentioned that a writer of Gibbon's standing found it of some value; for in the twenty-fifth chapter of his *History* he acknowledged in a note that he had chosen as his guides to Caledonian antiquity "two learned and ingenious Highlanders"; and he referred to the third edition of Macpherson's work, and to the minister of Sleat's *Dissertations.* In an advertisement prefixed to the second edition, Macpherson expressed his admiration for Mr. Whittaker's ingenuity and learning, but declared that he remained unconverted by his arguments. "I am," he went on to say, "tired of polemical writing, and I leave my system to its fate. Even my

[1] *Edinburgh Monthly Magazine*, Sept., 1810.
[2] See Nicholls' *Lit. Anecd.*, iii. 102.

vanity joins issue with my indolence. I hate
to fight without spectators." Nor did he
publish anything more about the Celts ; he
confined himself to discussing with his countrymen what he used to call "a dish of Gaelic".

His next venture was a translation of the
Iliad. This he is said to have executed in
the space of three months.[1] According to
his own account, the work was put upon
him by his Scotch friends, who conceived
that his performances with the remains of
Ossian well fitted him to render Homer into
attractive English. When they approached
him on the subject he was, as he tells us, at
first disinclined to undertake the work ; but
he was afterwards induced to do so by the
representations of a gentleman for whose judgment he professed a high respect. This gentleman had mentioned that he and others would
like to see parts of Homer translated in the
manner of *Fingal;* and to please him the trial
was made, and then continued.[2] Blair encouraged him to proceed. "I am exceedingly
glad," he wrote, "to hear that you have under-

[1] Laing, *op. cit.*, i. 41.
[2] Preface to the work.

taken Homer. Ferguson's idea that you were a proper person for such a work is not new. Ever since your translation of Ossian, we have often been saying the same in this country; and, if I mistake not, I have more than once told you so."[1]

The work was published early in 1773. Macpherson begged the public not to take his version for *mere prose*. He had, he said, measured the whole of it in his ear, guided in some degree by the original Greek, and, to bring the reader's eye to the assistance of his ear, he had marked the fall of the cadence by a short line, wherever there was no recognised stop. The effect is curious.

" The wrath of the son of Peleus—O goddess of song, unfold ! The deadly wrath of Achilles : to Greece the source of many woes ! Which peopled the regions of death—with shades of heroes untimely slain : while pale they lay along the shore : Torn by beasts and birds of prey : But such was the will of Jove ! Begin the verse, from the source of the rage between Achilles and the sovereign of men."

Some of Macpherson's Scotch friends were loud in their praise of the work. On 10th April,

[1] *Edinburgh Encycl.*, ed. David Brewster, 1830, s. v. " James Macpherson ".

Robertson, then principal of the University of Edinburgh, wrote him a letter full of compliments. "It is the only translation," he declared, "in which Homer appears like an ancient poet in his own simple magnificence. In all those passages where there is much elevation of expression or great power of description, the translation is very happy, and the force of the original is conveyed in beautiful and flowing language. I am persuaded that when the first rage and clamour of the English subsides, this will be the judgment universally received." [1]

But the "beautiful and flowing language" which impressed Robertson, himself master of the magniloquent style, was far removed from the simple vigour of the original. In the place of its concrete description, Macpherson betrayed the same tendency to the use of vague high-sounding phrases as had previously characterised his attempt on the old Highland ballads; and, indeed, his version of Homer throws no little light on the method of his earlier work. Hume wrote of it that he did not know whether the attempt or the execution were the worse, and in England it met with a mortifying recep-

[1] *Edinburgh Encycl.*

tion. In March, 1773, the *Critical Review* damned it with faint praise, but rebuked Macpherson for taking liberties with the original; and, by way of driving his criticism home, the reviewer gave a long list of the different ways in which Macpherson had rendered κορυθαίολος, the epithet of Hector. Some of his friends, notably Sir John Eliot, the physician, who carried it round to his patients, endeavoured to save it from ridicule; but it was everywhere asserted that Macpherson had done an audacious thing in parading Homer in a plaid and a kilt. Walpole laughed at it. "Macpherson," he wrote, "has been trying to prove how easy it is to make a Fingal out of Homer, after having tried to prove that Fingal was an original poem. But we live in an age of contradictions." [1]

The version of the *Iliad* was a mere by-work; and, whether it was good or bad, Macpherson set no store by it. He had a much more important undertaking in view. The booksellers were looking about them for some competent person willing to continue Hume's *History*, which, in spite of the early attack upon it, had in the end met with great success.

[1] Walpole's *Letters*, v. 444, 2nd March, 1773.

Hume had not carried his work beyond the Revolution; although he at first spoke of bringing it down to the accession of George I., and gave as his reason for concluding it there, not any fear of offence or danger, but a simple lack of materials. Afterwards, however, he held his hand at the year 1688; perhaps from a feeling that if he were to treat of subsequent events, he might find himself in the middle of political questions which were still burning; and that was not a prospect to be viewed with equanimity by a philosopher who respected his comfort. It had not yet occurred to the booksellers to take part of Smollett's hasty production as a supplement to Hume's work. The Jacobites were now in high favour at Court; and a historian who should treat of the reign of William III. from the Jacobite point of view would be sure of a sympathetic reception for his work. Macpherson was mentioned as a writer in all respects equal to the task; and the choice lay between him and Sir John Dalrymple of Cranstoun, who in his *Memoirs of Great Britain*, published in 1771 and 1773, had shown the spirit in which he regarded the Whigs. It was he who proved to the world that Algernon Sidney had been in

the pay of the French king ; but it was reserved
for Macpherson to make still more damaging
revelations.

Hume can hardly have been pleased when
Strahan wrote to tell him that either one or
other of these notorious Jacobites was likely
to continue his work. But we find him writing
good-humouredly to Strahan, and discussing the
merits of the rival candidates. " Macpherson,"
he said, "has style and spirit, but is hot-headed,
and consequently without judgment. The
knight has spirit but no style, and still less
judgment than the other."[1] To his friend
Adam Smith he was much more frank ; and
to him he roundly expressed the opinion that,
of all men of parts, Macpherson had "the most
anti-historical head in the universe ".[2]

Nevertheless, Macpherson put his hand to
the work in earnest ; he spared no pains in
the collection of his material ; and he produced
a volume which excited interest and astonishment. Some of Hume's material had been
taken from the papers left by the indefatigable

[1] 30th January, 1773. *Hume's Letters to William Strahan,*
ed. Birkbeck Hill.
[2] Burton's *Life,* ii. 467.

Thomas Carte, and Macpherson drew from the same source. In 1743 Carte, also a fervent Jacobite, had issued proposals for a complete history of civil life in England, for which he obtained a large number of subscribers, and made the most extensive research. But the time had not yet arrived when it was safe to present a picture of the Revolution in Jacobite colours; the rising of '45 intervened; and Carte fell a victim to the strength of his political sympathies. When his first volume appeared in 1747, it contained a reference to a case of king's evil, which, as Carte asserted, had been cured by the Pretender in France; and this unfortunate thrust brought the author and his work to the ground. Although he persevered and published two more volumes, the work was uncompleted at his death in 1754. Amongst the papers which he left was a series of valuable extracts from documents preserved in the Scots' College at Paris. Some of these Macpherson purchased from his widow for £300. He also derived great assistance from the use of some ten volumes of papers relating to the house of Brunswick, discovered and purchased by Matthew Duane.[1]

---

[1] Nicholls' *Lit. Anecd.*, ii. 574 ; iii. 497.

The papers which had formerly belonged to Carte consisted of extracts from the correspondence of Nairne, secretary for many years to the ministers of the exiled king and his son; and also of passages taken from memoirs of the king, written by himself. For the purpose of verifying these extracts and obtaining further information for himself, Macpherson in 1774 went to Paris, and examined the archives in the Scots' College. By the influence of Count Patullo and others at the Court of Versailles, he obtained an introduction to the Duc d'Aiguillon, the foreign minister.[1] Macpherson tells us that this nobleman gave him permission to inspect certain papers in the French Foreign Office, and while he was compelled to return to England before he could avail himself of it, he received some important information from that source. He also obtained material from MSS. in the Bodleian Library, and from private sources; although, as he tells us, he was refused permission to inspect other collections, both public and private.[2]

Macpherson determined to publish his ma-

---

[1] *Edinburgh Encyclopædia, loc. cit.*
[2] Macpherson's Preface to his *History of Great Britain*, etc.

terials before bringing out the *History* on which
it was based.   Nor was this step injudicious :
he was well aware that the facts which he was
about to give to the public would stir the embers
of a past struggle, and that in proving the later
intrigues of Marlborough with the Stuarts he
would be provoking the bitter resentment of the
Whigs.   Mindful of what had happened with a
previous production, he foresaw that the truth
of his information would be assailed, and he
himself denounced for the second time as an
impostor.   To forestall criticism, he left the
documents on view at his publishers', and early
in 1775 they were printed and issued as *Original
Papers containing the Secret History of Great
Britain from the Restoration to the Accession of
the House of Hannover, with Memoirs of James II·*
The Papers raised a storm of astonishment, and
the delight of the Tories was only equalled by
the disgust of the Whigs.   Walpole gave vent to
his feelings in the strongest language ; and even
in a later day the part which Macpherson played
in the work has always exposed him to Whig
contempt. [1]   It was not long before the assault

[1] For some remarks on the character and authenticity of
the Papers, see Ranke's *Hist. of Eng. in the 17th Cent.*, vi. 35.

which he expected was delivered. The authenticity of the Papers was impugned in *A Letter
from a Rustic,* who accused Macpherson of charg-
ing the ancestors of some of the best families in
England with the basest treachery, on the sole
affirmation of James' agents, who had their
own interest in persuading their master that he
would be received in England with acclamation
by Whigs and Tories alike. " Clear up the
mystery of Ossian," said this anonymous Whig,
" before you ask us to believe in Nairne."

At the same time he was attacked in the *St.
James' Chronicle* by a writer signing himself " A
Plain Dealer ". This called forth the only reply
which Macpherson seems to have made to his
critics, and it is sufficiently vigorous. His

Walpole wrote, on 14th April, 1775 : ''As for Macpherson,
I stopped dead short in the first volume : never was such a
heap of insignificant trash and lies." In his *Journal of the
Reign of George III.,* i. 472, he branded Macpherson and
Dalrymple as men whose common character destroyed all
belief in the credibility of their publications. They had, he
said, coined or manipulated alleged historical documents,
and then refused the families whom they defamed any opportunity of verification. Macaulay, in his *Hist. of Eng.,* chap.
x., note, declared that parts of the *Memoirs* were of the very
highest authority, but that the rest had no more value than
any common Jacobite pamphlet.

volume had been brought out by Strahan and
Cadell; and Cadell, it appears, had suggested
that some notice should be taken of the " Plain
Dealer".   The following undated letter to Cadell,
with an enclosure, has been preserved.   It was
probably written early in 1775.

" Private.

" Dear Sir,

        " Something like the enclosed may do.
Will you transcribe it carefully, as it would be
highly improper anything in commendation of
the *work* should go in the hand of the author?
I can easily trace the malignity of the John-
sonians in the 'Plain Dealer'.   Such allegations,
though too futile to impose on men of sense, may
have weight with the foolish and prejudiced, who
are a great majority of mankind.   I think, therefore, no such things should appear at all, if it can
be done.

        " I am, dear Sir,

                " Yours affectionately,

                        " J. M.

" Half-past 4 o'clock.
"To Mr. Cadell, bookseller, opposite Catherine
Street, Strand."

"' To the Printer of the *St. James' Chronicle.*
"' It is doubtful whether the writer who
signs himself " A Plain Dealer " in your paper
of Tuesday discovers most malice or folly.   He

presumes to call in question the authenticity of the Papers just published by Mr. Macpherson ; yet the originals have lain for these two months past in the hands of Mr. Cadell, the bookseller, for the inspection of the public. The insinuations of the " Plain Dealer" concerning the principles of the writer are as false as his allegations against the authenticity of the Papers. The impartiality of Mr. Macpherson's narration, his undeviating attention to truth, his strict justice to the characters of men, the liberality of his observations on facts, and his apparent and uniform attachment to the rights of human nature (the great foundation of civil liberty), have met with the unanimous approbation of the judicious and unprejudiced of all parties. If he is not a favourite with the violent of any party, it is because he is biassed by the follies of none.

" ' IMPARTIAL.' " [1]

Later in the same year Macpherson brought out his *History of Great Britain from the Restoration to the Accession of the House of Hannover;* but its effect had been in some measure discounted by the previous appearance of the Papers. Hume was unable to form a high opinion of the work ; he told Strahan that it was one of the most wretched productions that

---

[1] Published in the *Academy*, 19th Oct., 1878.

ever came from his press.[1] It was, however, successful, and soon entered a second edition. The publishers gave Macpherson £3000 for the copyright.[2]

---

[1] *Hume's Letters to Strahan,* 13th Nov., 1775.
[2] *Edinburgh Encyclopædia, loc. cit.*

CHAPTER XI.

Macpherson's Social Position. — His Scotch Friends.—Gibbon's Criticism.—New Edition of the Poems.—Johnson in Scotland.—The Quarrel with Johnson.—The Originals.—Further Controversy.

About this time Macpherson was employed on behalf of the Court to supervise the newspapers, and to use what influence he could to prevent attacks on the Government. For this he received a salary of £600 a year.[1] He was becoming well-to-do; and with his literary reputation, the favour of the great, and his own social talents, he soon made his way in the world of London. When he was in town he lived in Westminster, in a street then known as Manchester Buildings, chiefly inhabited by bachelor members of parliament and journalists;[2] but he also possessed

[1] Walpole's *Journal*, ii. 17.

[2] It was a double set of private houses, extending in a southerly direction between Cannon Row and the river, on the site now occupied by the St. Stephen's Club and the Westminster Station on the District Railway. (See Thornbury's *Old and New London*, iii. 381.)

a small villa on Putney Common, to which he
often retired. It was there that he entertained
his friends. He was now a handsome man, of a
fair and somewhat florid complexion, with a full
countenance, both sensitive and acute, and betraying a temperament by no means ascetic.
Whenever he appeared in the *salons* of the blue-
stockings, or in the Pantheon, or took the air
in the Mall, or mingled with the crowd in the
Gardens of Ranelagh or Vauxhall, he could hardly
fail to be a conspicuous figure, for he stood six
feet three in his boots.[1] We have two portraits
of him. In June, 1772, when he was in his
thirty-sixth year, he had sat to Reynolds, and
the portrait then produced, representing him in
a fur-edged coat with a scroll in his hand, is that
by which he is best known;[2] the other, by
Romney, is the more pleasing of the two.
It forms the frontispiece to this volume.

On the question of the authenticity of the
poems, Macpherson still maintained his attitude of proud reserve. The unvarnished account
which Blair afterwards gave of his character

---

[1] R. Carruthers' *Highland Note Book*, 305-312 (Edinb.,
1843).

[2] Leslie and Taylor's *Life of Reynolds*, i. 465.

finds, perhaps, its most fitting application at this period of his career ; and it must be remembered that Blair had a lengthy acquaintance with Macpherson, had taken a very warm interest in his work, and stands clear of any suspicion of adverse prejudice. He describes him as proud, high-spirited, and disdainful; irritable to a degree when his honour and veracity were impeached ; not very apt on any occasion to listen to advice ; and most obstinate in his determination to disregard any censure which he thought unjust, and to pay no attention to those who opposed him or cavilled at him.[1] But Macpherson may also have maintained his reserve, because he perceived that the air of mystery in which his work was now enveloped, was exciting an adventitious interest in the man who had produced it. In spite of predictions to the contrary, the poems were becoming increasingly popular, both in England and on the continent, as is shown by the many attempts that were made to turn them into verse.[2] The Scotch became proud of a work

[1] *Rep.*, App., 61.

[2] The *Songs of Selma* had been immediately versified, as appears by an announcement in the *British Magazine* for February, 1762. As early as June of that year, Samuel

which was in a sense national, and it began to
be asserted that every line of it was authentic.
Smollett, for instance, in his *Humphrey Clinker*
made one of the characters declare that the
poems of Ossian were in every mouth in the
Highlands.[1] There is some ground for believ-
ing that it was about this time that a wild
scheme was broached in Kingussie for an ex-
hibition of paintings in illustration of the works
of Ossian. It was to be conducted on a plan
similar to that of a Shakespearean Gallery of
the day; a new building was to be constructed
in a central situation in London ; the greatest

Derrick, a miscellaneous writer, had put parts of *Fingal*
into verse. John Wodrow, minister of Islay, published in
1769 a versification of *Carthon, The Death of Cuchullin*, and
Darthula, and in 1771 of *Fingal*, which also appeared in
heroics at Warrington in 1776. The first foreign translation
was into Italian verse by Cesarotti in 1763 ; the next, in
1764, into German prose by Engelbrecht and Wittenberg,
and into German verse in 1768-9 by Michel Denis, an
Austrian Jesuit. Goethe began his translation in 1770. A
French translation of *Temora* appeared in 1774. Thus at
this period of Macpherson's life, the poems were well known
all over Western Europe.

[1] *Humphrey Clinker*, 3rd Sept. " A famous antiquarian
of this country, the laird of Macfarlane, at whose house we
dined, can repeat them all in the original Gaelic." Smollett's
work was at once assailed as a defence of the Scotch.

artists of the age were to be employed; and elaborate calculations were made to prove that it would be a highly successful investment for spare capital.[1] It does not appear Macpherson had anything to do with it.

He received frequent visits from his Scotch friends, and to them, on the subject of Ossian, he was always communicative. Dr. Carlyle relates that during the winters of 1769 and 1770, which he spent in London, he was on very intimate terms with Macpherson, and saw him daily. " I never was able," wrote Carlyle,

" to discover in his most unguarded moments that he was any other than the collector and translator of the works of Ossian, or assumed any other merit than might be derived from thence. But I have heard him express the greatest contempt and disdain for those who thought him the fabricator of them. If there was any person who asserted that Macpherson had owned it to himself, even that would not shake my faith; for I knew him to be of a temper, when he was teased and fretted, to carry his indignation that far."[2]

Captain Morison and John Home were, at various times, much in his company in

[1] See Mr. Alex. Macpherson, *op. cit.*, p. 205.
[2] *Rep.*, App., 68.

London. Blair also came to see him ; but it is not recorded that he remained on very intimate terms with his former disciple. There was something in Macpherson's life in London with which Blair could hardly be expected to sympathise. He once asked Macpherson why he lived in England, as he certainly could not be fond of John Bull. " Sir," said he, " I hate John Bull, but I love his daughters."[1]

From time to time the poems encountered fair criticism. In 1773 Gibbon drew the attention of the learned to an anachronism in the account of the Roman invasion, where the son of the Emperor Severus, who figured as " the King of the World," was designated Caracul. At the time of the war, he was known as Antoninus ; and it was strange, said Gibbon, that the Highland bard should describe him by a nickname not invented until four years later, and not commonly used by the Romans before the emperor's death.[2] He sent this criticism

[1] *Boswelliana.*

[2] Gibbon afterwards re-stated this criticism in the first vol. of his *History* (1776), chap. vi., where he descants, with his fine irony, on "the pleasing supposition that Fingal lived and that Ossian sung". But he did not avow any positive disbelief in the general authenticity of the poems ; and in

to Whittaker, who sagaciously replied that as
Antoninus came to be generally known by his
nickname it might have been used, and indeed
would naturally have been used, in any poems
about him ; and that this anachronism would
not in itself invalidate their authenticity.[1]

In 1773 Macpherson wrote a new preface to
his work, which was then entering on a fourth
edition ; and he took the opportunity of altering
and improving it in accordance with various sug-
gestions that had been made to him. Lord
Kaimes, for instance, tells us[2] that in 1771 he
wrote to Macpherson, to call his attention to
several imperfections ; particularly the confusion
of names, and the want of proper order in the
relation of incidents ; and he recommended a
fresh arrangement of the poems, and some
amendment of the style. He records that
Macpherson embraced his hints more readily
than he had expected. The translator's attitude to the public, his contempt of adverse

his fifteenth chapter, in describing the spread of Christianity,
he made a serious reference to Macpherson's *Dissertations*.

[1] Gibbon's *Misc. Works*, ed. 1814, ii. 101.

[2] *Memoirs of Henry Home, Lord Kaimes*, by A. F.
Tytler, ii. 122.

criticism, and his good opinion of his own abilities, will be obvious in the following extracts from the new preface :—

" The eagerness with which these poems have been received abroad are a recompence for the coldness with which a few have affected to treat them at home. All the polite nations of Europe have transferred them into their respective languages ; and they speak of him who brought them to light in terms that might flatter the vanity of one fond of fame. . . .

" Though the taste which defines genius by the points of the compass is a fit subject for mirth in itself, it is often a serious matter in the sale of a work. When rivers define the limits of abilities, as well as the boundaries of countries, a writer may measure his success by the latitude under which he was born. It was to avoid a part of this inconvenience that the author is said by some, who speak without any authority, to have ascribed his own productions to another name. If this was the case, he was but young in the art of deception. When he placed the poet in antiquity, the translator should have been born on this side of the Tweed. . . .

" One of the chief improvements in this edition is the care taken in arranging the poems in the order of time, so as to form a kind of regular history of the age to which they relate. The writer has now resigned them for ever to their fate. . . . Through the medium of version upon version, they retain in foreign languages their native character of simplicity and energy. Genuine poetry, like gold, loses little, when properly transfused ;

but when a composition cannot bear the test
of a literal version, it is a counterfeit which
ought not to pass current. The operation
must, however, be performed with skilful
hands. A translator who cannot equal his
original is incapable of expressing its beauties."

The meaning of this last sentence is perfectly
obvious ; and, in spite of its vanity, it contains a
profound truth. But some over-zealous critics
have tortured it into a subtle confession, on the
part of the writer, that he was, after all, an
author and not a translator.

While Macpherson was bringing out the fourth
edition of the poems, Johnson was making his
tour in Scotland, and working himself up for a
public attack upon their authenticity. It was
some ten years now since he had first abused
them to his friends ; and in the meantime he
seems to have held his peace. It is possible that
his abuse was silenced for a while by the effect
of the Highland testimony ; for Blair, in the letter
to Hume already cited,[1] declared that he had
converted " that barbarian, Sam. Johnson," who,
as Lord Elibank reported, owned himself convinced. But if Johnson was ever converted, he
soon returned to his former opinion, and he went

[1] See *supra*, p. 210.

to the Highlands firmly persuaded that the poems
were a gross fraud. He had, it is true, so far
modified his earlier contempt as to admit that
they contained some passages from old songs, and
names that circulated in popular stories ; but
that made no difference in his estimate of their
value. In this temper he bethought himself of
investigating the authenticity of the poems on
the spot ; and although he was entirely ignorant
of Gaelic, he made ready to hear recitations, to
search for manuscripts, and to determine the character and history of the language. He quickly
reached the conclusion that he must draw a distinction between Gaelic and Irish, but that Gaelic,
or Earse, as he called it, never was a written language, and that the world did not contain an Earse
manuscript a hundred years old. As for the
bards and senachies, he decided from what he
heard that they had for centuries ceased to exist;
and that the bard, when he did exist, was "a
barbarian among barbarians, who, knowing nothing himself, lived with others that knew no
more ". Johnson received, as he acknowledged,
great kindness and courtesy at the hands of Dr.
Macqueen, the minister of Kilmuir, who had
given Blair his positive testimony to the authen-

ticity of such parts of Macpherson's work as
had been recited in his hearing; but he told
Macqueen flatly that he did not believe his own
testimony, although he was very willing that the
world should believe it. When Macqueen took
no notice of this affront, Johnson supposed himself to have hit the right nail upon the head;
" he wished me," said he, " to be deceived for the
honour of his country, but would not directly
and formally deceive me ". Having browbeaten
his unfortunate host, Johnson made up his mind
that the whole of the testimony which Blair had
adduced was a national conspiracy in falsehood,
and consoled himself with the reflection that
" a Scotchman must be a very sturdy moralist
who does not love Scotland better than truth ".[1]

These and similar observations Johnson proceeded to set down in a volume recording his
travels in the Highlands. It was delivered to
his publishers Strahan and Cadell in the summer
of 1774; and by October of that year, the rumour
began to spread that it was to contain a vigorous
attack on Macpherson and his poems. [2] The

---

[1] Johnson's *Journey to the Western Islands of Scotland*,
pp. 267-276.

[2] See Walpole's *Letters*, vi. 119, where Mason speaks of
the rumour.

news reached Macpherson in all likelihood
through Strahan, who was his intimate friend;
for when the volume was in print he was informed of the exact words in which Johnson
intended to speak of him.   One passage ran as
follows :—

> "I suppose my opinion of the poems of
> Ossian is already discovered. I believe they
> never existed in any other form than that which
> we have seen. The editor, or author, could
> never show the original; nor can it be shown
> by any other. To revenge reasonable incredulity
> by refusing evidence is a degree of insolence
> with which the world is not yet acquainted; and
> stubborn audacity is the last refuge of guilt."

Goldsmith said of Johnson, with great truth,
that although he had a roughness in his manner,
no man alive had a more tender heart; "he had
nothing of the bear but the skin". The skin
was all that he showed to Macpherson. On
the question of authenticity Johnson's declaration was a mere piece of ignorant dogmatism,
and Macpherson was well aware that he could
afford to let it pass; but he was angry at the
language which Johnson thought fit to apply to
him, and as the affront was entirely unprovoked,
it can hardly be said that he did wrong to be

angry. Strahan, it appears, shared this view of the matter; and as Strahan was his publisher as well as Johnson's, Macpherson took the very proper and dignified step of sending him a letter of protest, to be shown to Johnson, in the hope that that eminent man might be disposed to moderate his language.

"Private.

"Dear Sir,

"Upon mature consideration, I have sent the enclosed *ostensible letter*. However unwilling I may be, *at this time especially*, to do anything that may create noise, I find I cannot pass over the expressions contained in Dr. Johnson's pamphlet. I desire, therefore, that you will use your endeavours with that *impertinent fellow* to induce him to soften the expressions concerning me, though it should occasion the loss of a few days in the publication. If he has a grain of common-sense, I suppose he will see the impropriety of the words, and prevent further trouble. You may show to him the enclosed, but to none else; and take care to keep it in your own hands.

"I am, dear Sir,

"Yours affectionately,

"J. MACPHERSON.

"Manchester Buildings, Jan. 15, 1775."

The enclosure was couched in polite terms; and if there was any dissimulation in its tone, some excuse may be found for it in Macpherson's desire to do his duty to Strahan as well as to be polite to Johnson.

" Dear Sir,

" A friend of mine has this moment put into my hands a sentence from a work entitled *A Journey to the Western Islands of Scotland,* which, I am informed, is written by Dr. Johnson. In expressing his incredulity with regard to the authenticity of the poems of Ossian he makes use of the words *insolence, audacity,* and *guilt.* To his want of belief on this subject I have not the smallest objection. But I suppose you will agree with me, that such expressions ought not to be used by one gentleman to another ; and that whenever they are used, they cannot be passed over with impunity. To prevent consequences that may be at once disagreeable to Dr. Johnson and to myself, I desire the favour that you will wait upon him, and tell him that I *expect* he will cancel from the *Journal* the *injurious expressions* above mentioned. I hope that, upon cool reflection, he will be of opinion that this expectation of mine is not unreasonable.

" I am, dear Sir,

" Your most obedient humble servant,

" JAMES MACPHERSON.[1]

" Manchester Buildings, Jan. 15, 1775.

" William Strahan, Esq."

[1] These letters were printed in the *Academy,* Oct. 19, 1878.

But the book was printed and ready for publication, and Macpherson was informed that no part of it could now be cancelled. He was then sanguine enough to send another message to Johnson, with a proposal that a slip should be inserted in the volume, disclaiming any desire to give offence. The following hasty letter to Strahan is undated, but it must have followed immediately on the preceding one.

" Private.

" Dear Sir,

"As I expect to have Dr. Johnson's final answer to my, I think, very just demands, at seven o'clock, I beg leave to enclose to you the purport of such an Advertisement as would satisfy me. As I am *very serious* upon this business I insist that you will keep it to yourself ; for were it not [for] the present circumstances of an affair, in which you (as well as I) are concerned, I should before this time have *traced out* the author of this journey in a very *effectual* manner. Unless I have a satisfactory answer, I am determined (indeed, it is necessary) to bring that business to a *conclusion* before I *begin* any other.

" I am, dear Sir,
" Yours, etc., etc.,
" J. MACPHERSON.[1]

" Past 4 o'clock."

[1] *Academy*, Oct. 19, 1878. The other " affair " here mentioned is not improbably the publication of the *Original Papers*, which Strahan was at this time about to issue.

The " Advertisement " was in these terms :—

" The author of the *Journey to the Western Islands of Scotland*, finding, when it was too late to make any alterations, that some expressions in page   and   have given offence to the gentleman alluded to, he takes this method of informing the public, that he meant no personal reflection; and that should this work come to a second impression, he will take care to expunge such words as seem, though undesignedly, to convey an affront. This is a piece of justice which the author owes to himself as well as to that gentleman."

Johnson had already received copies of his work, and was distributing them to his friends;[1] but whatever response he may have made to this proposal, there is no evidence that he felt any concern, on his own or on Macpherson's behalf, in regard to the violent language which he had used. Now that a polite protest had failed of any effect, Macpherson angrily adopted the example which Johnson had set him. He threw all courtesy aside, and wrote to the dictator that " his age and infirmities alone protected him from the treatment due to an infamous liar and

[1] See letter to Boswell, dated January 14, 1775, in which he writes of having sent a copy to the king. (Boswell's *Life*, æt. 66.)

traducer ".[1] Johnson had specifically charged him with "revenging reasonable incredulity by refusing evidence"; and Macpherson lost no time in doing what he could to refute the public accusation that had been made. He called upon Becket, his former publisher, to show that the charge was false; and Becket then sent the following statement to the papers :—

"To the Public.

"DOCTOR JOHNSON having asserted in his late publication that the TRANSLATOR OF OSSIAN'S POEMS 'never could show the original, nor can it be shown by any other,' I hereby declare that the originals of *Fingal* and other poems of Ossian lay in my shop for many months in the year 1762, for the inspection of the curious. The public were not only apprised of their lying there for inspection, but even proposals for publishing the originals of the poems of Ossian were dispersed through the kingdom, and advertised in the newspapers. Upon finding that a number of subscribers sufficient to bear the expenses were not likely to appear, I returned the manuscript to the proprietor, in whose hands they still remain.

"THOMAS BECKET.[2]

" Adelphi, 19th January, 1775."

[1] This description of Macpherson's first letter is taken from Clark's answer to Shaw's *Inquiry*, p. 48. Clark there gives the words on the authority of a friend.

[2] See *Notes and Queries*, II. iii. 28.

It was now some thirteen years since the MSS. had been exhibited. Johnson was as deaf to Becket's testimony as he was indifferent to Macpherson's anger. Nor was he at all moved by a formal challenge from his adversary.[1] Having purchased a formidable cudgel, six feet in length, and ending in a knob three inches in diameter, he addressed Macpherson in the following terms :—

" Mr. James Macpherson,

" I received your foolish and impudent note. Whatever insult is offered me, I will do my best to repel, and what I cannot do for myself, the law shall do for me. I will not desist from detecting what I think a cheat, from any fear of the menaces of a Ruffian.

" What would you have me retract? I thought your book an imposture ; I think it an imposture still. For this opinion I have given my reasons to the public, which I here dare you refute. Your rage I defy. Your abilities, since your Homer, are not so formidable ; and what I hear of your morals inclines me to pay regard, not to what you shall say, but to what you shall prove. You may print this if you will.

" SAM. JOHNSON.[2]

" 20th January, 1775."

[1] The gentleman who carried it, William Duncan, asserted the fact in a letter to Sir John Sinclair. See Sinclair, *op. cit.*, i. ccxx.

[2] The original of this well-known letter was sold by

Such were the incidents of a famous quarrel. When Walpole heard of it he fastidiously declared that Macpherson had been as much a bully as Johnson a brute.[1]

It remains to show in what spirit Johnson spoke of the encounter to his friends. We find him writing to Boswell, who was then in Edinburgh, to say that Macpherson was very furious, and to ask for further intelligence about him and his *Fingal.* "Do what you can," he urged, "and do it quickly. Is Lord Hailes on our side?" Boswell replied that his friend's conduct had been represented in a very unfavourable light in Edinburgh, and begged Johnson to furnish him with a sufficient answer. He also inquired what Becket meant by the statement about the originals. To this inquiry Johnson, it seems, returned no answer ; but he expressed surprise that Boswell, "knowing the disposition of his countrymen to tell lies in favour of one another," should have been affected by any reports

auction in 1875, for £50. The copy which appears in Boswell's *Life* was dictated by Johnson from recollection; and the words of the first paragraph are not quite the same as those given above, which are taken from the printed form in the auctioneer's catalogue. [1] *Journal,* i. 472.

that circulated amongst them.   Macpherson, he declared, had never offered him any evidence of any kind, but only thought of intimidating him by noise and threats.

" The state of the question is this.   He and Dr. Blair, whom I consider as deceived, say that he copied the poems from old manuscripts.   His copies, if he had them, and I believe him to have none, are nothing.   Where are the manuscripts ? They can be shown if they exist, and they never were shown. . . . A nation that cannot write, or a language that was never written, has no manuscripts.

"But whatever he has, he never offered to show. If old manuscripts should now be mentioned, I should, unless there were more evidence than can easily be had, suppose them another proof of Scotch conspiracy in national falsehood.   Do not censure the expression ; you know it to be true." [1]

Macpherson had not said that he copied the poem from old manuscripts, but that he had put it together out of fragments, some of them taken from manuscripts, and some from oral recitation ; and Johnson, as appears by his own statements, never examined the prefaces and the notes in which Macpherson had explained the nature of his work.   Boswell wrote

[1] 7th February, 1775.

that one or two well-known Highland gentlemen possessed several manuscripts containing
Erse poetry, apparently very ancient, and that,
if proper means were used, the inquiry was
not yet quite hopeless. Johnson, however,
would hear nothing of them ; even if these
manuscripts were fifty or even a hundred
years old, there was no proof that they, too,
were not forged. From what he had heard,
Macpherson had translated part of his work
into Gaelic, taught a boy to write it, and
directed him to say that he had learned it
of his grandmother. "You know how little
a Highlander can be trusted. Macpherson is,
so far as I know, very quiet. Is not that
proof enough ? Everything is against him."

Macpherson did no more ; and at the time
there was nothing more for him to do but to
print the originals as he had them. The originals
were confessedly a collection of disconnected
fragments ; and the mere labour of arranging
and editing them for the press was not a work
to be undertaken in haste, even if there had been
no vexed questions to be solved in the matter
of Gaelic orthography, or no difficulties to be
apprehended with subscribers, publishers and

printers. The leisure which he enjoyed from his political employment was devoted to his *History*, and the attack had been made upon him at the very moment when he was completing this work and seeing his *Original Papers* through the press. Nor can it be said that if he had printed his collection of fragments at this time, they would have been likely to have much effect on critics ignorant of Gaelic and interested in maintaining an attitude of hostility. Most of his Scotch and many of his English friends were perfectly satisfied as to the general authenticity of the poems, and those of them who had watched him at his work of translation fifteen years previously had never raised any doubts of his honesty. It seems, however, that now or shortly afterwards he gave a definite promise to some of his friends to print the originals, as soon as he should have time to arrange them, and provided that the expense of publication could be met.

The news of the encounter with Johnson was soon spread abroad, and the controversy was carried on in the periodicals of the day. Some of them took Macpherson's part and others took his opponent's, and on both sides there was much abuse. An instance of the more educated argument may be found in a letter signed " W. Cambrensis " in the *St. James' Chronicle,* 23rd March, 1775 ; where the writer, adverting to Johnson's statement in his *Journey* that no long poems could be handed down by tradition, said that the doctor must remember boys at school who could easily repeat a whole book of Virgil. There were, he declared, several persons in Wales who could repeat long poems attributed to Taliesin, who flourished at a period not much less remote than that assigned to the Scottish bard.

From the newspapers the controversy soon found its way into pamphlets, and in 1779 from pamphlets into books ; but in the absence of the originals, and in the general ignorance of Gaelic language and literature, the kind of reasoning employed at the time was of no very edifying character, and without any illuminating results. Nor is it necessary to do much more than mention the books in which the controversy was for two or three years fiercely maintained. In 1779 there appeared in London *Remarks on Dr. Johnson's Tour,* in which the writer, a Scotchman named Macnicol, essayed the easy task of following

Johnson through his journey and making sport
of his observations. Incidentally he brought in
abundant evidence of the fact that there were
many old Gaelic manuscripts in the possession
of various gentlemen in the Highlands, whose
names he gave. Some of the abuse of Johnson,
as the writer afterwards declared, was inserted
without his knowledge when the book was being
printed in London; and suspicion pointed to
Macpherson as the author of it. This was never
proved; and as Johnson had many enemies in
London besides Macpherson, it would be difficult to prove it; moreover, we know that whatever Macpherson may have written on Johnson
in private, he refrained from making any public
attack upon him.[1]

Macnicol's work was answered in 1781, in a
small volume entitled *An Inquiry into the Authenticity of the Poems ascribed to Ossian,* by William
Shaw, also a Scotchman, and author of a Gaelic
grammar and dictionary. Shaw was by all
accounts not only a poor Gaelic scholar but
also a man of low character, who had been

---

[1] See Carruthers, *op. cit.* Many coarse lampoons and
epigrams on Johnson existed amongst Macpherson's papers
at the time of his death.

compelled to decamp from a school which he had carried on at Glenorchay. He professed to have shaken off all national bigotry, and by some fulsome adulation he attracted the attention of Johnson. When a violent personal attack was made upon Shaw by one Clark, of Edinburgh, Johnson took Shaw under his protection and helped him to write a rejoinder, which appeared in 1782.[1] The controversy thereupon began to wane, and in 1785 Boswell declared that public interest in it had come to an end.[2]

[1] Boswell's *Life* (æt. 74).
[2] Boswell's *Journal of a Tour to the Hebrides*, Nov. 10.

CHAPTER XII.

Macpherson as a Pamphleteer.—Assists Sir John Macpherson in Attacking the East India Company. — Reviews the Conduct of the Opposition.—Letters on the Threatened Invasion. — Irish and Indian Affairs.—Becomes Member for Camelford.—Agent for the Nabob of Arcot. — Rise in his Fortunes. — The Ossianic Controversy Again.—The Indian Subscription.

As a writer in the service of Lord North's Ministry, Macpherson found plenty of employment for his pen in the political questions of the day, which were certainly of the most absorbing character. At home there were constitutional struggles, religious entanglements, and Irish difficulties beyond the common measure. The position abroad was disastrous. The enmity of France and of Spain had become a permanent trouble; the American colonies, chafing for ten years under desultory taxation, were on the point of declaring their independence; and while in India, as though to compensate for loss in the

(258)

West, the supremacy had lately been won, those
who were laying the foundations of empire were
now reaping the fruits of conquest with a
rapacity that aroused the bitterest antagonism
of their own countrymen.

It was the American policy of the Government which called for the most strenuous support,
and placed the heaviest burden on its adherents ;
not so much from the gravity of the issues at
stake, as from the uncompromising opposition of
the Whigs, who carried their disapproval so far
that for some time they refused to attend Parliament except for private business. When in
July, 1776, the thirteen colonies issued their
famous Declaration, Macpherson was employed
by the Ministry to write a popular reply. In
*The Rights of Great Britain asserted against
the Claims of America*, he produced a pamphlet
which quickly gained the ear of the public. It
went through many editions; nor can his friends
have failed to be pleased that it met with a
much greater success than attended Johnson's
efforts in his rancorous philippic, *Taxation No
Tyranny*, issued in the previous year. In supporting the American policy of the Government,
Macpherson was acting in unison with most

of the Scotchmen prominent in London; for
although the Government failed to obtain addresses in its favour from any of the chief
cities in Scotland, the writers and politicians of
that country were as a rule on its side.[1]

But in 1777 a new, and, as it proved, a lucrative channel was opened to Macpherson's energy
in the tortuous business of Indian politics.   He
was at first drawn to it by his interest in the
affairs of his kinsman John Macpherson, son of
the minister of Sleat.   Early in life this remarkable man had gone out in the train of many
other adventurers to seek his fortune in India ;
he had become the servant of Mohammed Ali,
the nabob of Arcot ; and he was employed by
that potentate on the most confidential business.
The nabob was in many difficulties.   For a number of years he had been dependent on the favour
and protection of the East India Company ;
but neither its favour nor its protection had
availed to help him against the rapacity of some
of the Company's servants, who were amassing
great fortunes by private enterprise.   It was at
their instigation, or else with the sole object of
plunder, that he had twice invaded the neigh-

[1] See Mr. Lecky's *History*, iii. 534.

bouring territory of Tanjore, where he imprisoned the rajah on the pretext of forcing him to
pay his debts. The Company had interfered
in the dispute with a view to its own advantage; and by reckless promises to the Company's servants the nabob found himself and
his country under an enormous burden of debt.
It was hardly strange that of the nature and
justice of this debt different views were taken
by the nabob himself, the officials whom he
employed, the Court of Directors at home, and
the executive Government. In 1777, the nabob
resolved to appeal to the English Ministry to
help him in his difficulties; basing his hopes,
as it appears, on North's Regulation Act, which
four years previously had introduced some order
into the dealings between the English and the
natives. He entrusted the mission to his young
Scotch friend, who had recently been dismissed
by the Madras Council on suspicion of stirring
up the Government against the Company.

On his return to England John Macpherson
was kindly received by North, who formed
a high opinion of his abilities, and tried to
obtain his services at home. He had brought
with him various papers and letters in sup-

port of the nabob's case, to be laid before
the Directors ; and it was probably by North's
advice that he resolved to entrust the editing of
the papers and the preparation of the case to a
writer of acknowledged ability. The task fell to
Macpherson. With the help of his kinsman the
papers were arranged and printed before the end
of the year. They appeared as *Letters from
Mohammed Ali Chan, Nabob of Arcot, to the Court
of Directors.* To this was annexed *A Statement
of Facts relative to Tanjore.* The papers on
which the publication was based were set out
in an appendix.

Macpherson was interested in a work which
gave him an insight into the way in which the
business of politics was being managed in India ;
and it also showed him something of the method
pursued by a class of adventurers who were
then exciting no small disgust in English society.
The "nabobs," as they were called—the men
who from obscure beginnings had contrived to
possess themselves in a very short time of
enormous wealth, and had returned to spend
in arrogant display what they had obtained by
pillage and oppression, found themselves by a
happy fate the most unpopular men in the

country. To reveal to the public at home some of the doings of the East India Company was an undertaking attractive in itself; in the prevailing state of opinion it was sure to win sympathy; and an undertaking of this kind was, it appears, planned by the nabob's emissary. In 1779 there appeared *The History and Management of the East India Company, from its Origin in 1600 to the Present Times.* Of this work only one volume was published, containing, as the title declared, " the affairs of the Carnatic, in which the rights of the nabob are explained, and the injustice of the Company proved ". It was an anonymous publication; but while the work is commonly attributed to Macpherson, it is more than probable that a great part of it was written by his kinsman. But Macpherson gave him all the assistance in his power, and wrote the preface. It was there stated that the history was compiled from the facts published in the Directors' original papers, and other documents of equal authority which had been placed in the writer's hands by an official of the Crown, together with various private letters and communications. The labour of composition, added the writer, was long and tedious; " for the wading through

the sink of East India corruption and mis-
management is a task which adds disgust to
toil ".

But while he was thus engaged, Macpherson's
attention to politics at home was in no way
relaxed. He was still supervising the newspapers attached to the Government, and writing
pamphlets. To his utterance on the American
Declaration he now issued a counterpart, in
which he reviewed the conduct of the Whigs in
regard to the war. In 1778 the Opposition
was loudly expressing the opinion that the
colonists should be left independent. But in
the same year France made a treaty with the
States, and prepared to join in a great attack on
the English power. But for the bitterness roused
by this intervention, the struggle with America
would have been sooner abandoned. The nation,
however, was now involved in difficulties which
menaced its very existence, and an attempt was
made to present a show of unity by the introduction of a small Whig element into the Government; but, mainly perhaps through the efforts of
Burke, it failed. While we can now see that the
Opposition was right in the main, its conduct
at this juncture was sufficiently exposed to hos-

tile criticism. Macpherson's pamphlet, *A Short History of the Opposition during the last Session,* was issued anonymously in 1779, by Cadell, at the price of one shilling. It was well received; and the merit of the work caused it at the time to be ascribed to Gibbon, who was then one of North's supporters in the House of Commons.

In the summer of that year the combined French and Spanish fleets were cruising in the Channel, and threatening an invasion. There was a great alarm; the militia were called out, volunteers were hastily enrolled and drilled, and all the cattle and draught horses on the coasts were driven inland. A glimpse of the way in which this exciting news was received in London is afforded by the following letters from Macpherson to John Home :—

" Tuesday, two o'clock, August 17, 1779.

" My dear Sir,

"I have news to tell you. The French and Spanish fleets are at the mouth of the Channel. An express arrived this morning, a lieutenant of the *Marlborough,* of sixty-four guns, which ship was chased by the enemy to within a few leagues of the Lizard. Sir Charles Hardy was by the last accounts off Ushant. I reckon it likely that he has them between him and the land. The lieutenant says that an action must

have happened.   A general anxiety prevails, but
less than you could have supposed.   Our *friends*
look a little blue.   The times are big with events.
I have no doubt of our beating them ; unless the
same devil who turmoiled the 27th of July, 1778,
has still his black hand at our admiral's helm.
The express counted sixty-three sail, 'tis said,
of the line ; I hope sixty-three was the number
of the whole.   Should any new lights come ere
the post sets out, you may be put to the expense
of another ninepence.   We may probably demand the swords of the S. Fencibles in this
part of the world.

" Yours very affectionately,

" JAMES MACPHERSON."

" Tuesday, two o'clock, August 31.

"Nothing new of the fleets.   By the last
official accounts, the C. d'Orvilliers, with fifty of
the line, had advanced to where Sir Charles
Hardy had been left, on the 19th.   Our fleet had
been driven further west.   'Twas thought Sir
Charles was on another tack, and about twelve
leagues off. . . . We think here that Hardy ought
to beat 'em ; others say, he will miss them and
gain the Channel.   I am not under great apprehensions ; and John Bull keeps up his spirits
wonderfully.   All is calm, tranquil, and easy
here.   The Stocks don't fall ; and all the animal
functions, and even pleasures, go on as usual.
We shall hear some news soon.   'Tis a time of
anxious suspense to speculative men."

" September 3, 1779.

" This morning an express from Sir C. Hardy.
He was coming up Channel—the combined fleet

behind, it is said, under a press of sail, in pursuit.
The fogs, which prevailed at the mouth of the
Channel during the east wind, prevented their
meeting. All was involved in night. They
mutually heard the signal guns, but could not
see each other. We expect a decisive action.
I am not of that opinion. John Bull is perfectly
indifferent. Stocks rise; yet the fate of the
kingdom may depend on the turning up of the
die. One is disgusted with the white lies of the
day. I believe the Bourbons are serious. Johnston's fifty-gun *Romney* is thrown out of the line.
Hardy is in great spirits,—so is the whole fleet.
But, if we look back through time, we never had
a sea-advantage over France but with superiority
of numbers. I hope to announce a victory in my
next. The times are critical. A defeat would
involve us in confusion. I don't think that
drilling business ought to be *your* province in
these times. The battle will happen, perhaps, at
Spithead. Though I ought to know many things,
they communicate nothing. The bellman is at
the door." [1]

In Ireland, notwithstanding that in recent
years the severity of the commercial code had
been slightly modified and Catholic disabilities
largely relieved, there was still great resentment at the continued restrictions on trade;
and the general discontent was undoubtedly

[1] *Life of John Home*, by Henry Mackenzie, i., App., 139
et seq.

stirred by the action of French and American emissaries.   In the inability of the executive to leave troops in Ireland, a large
body of volunteers had been enrolled for the
protection of the coast; and although the
body showed the most exemplary loyalty, its
existence was a powerful argument in favour
of allaying a discontent that had become
dangerous, and of annulling most of the restrictions which oppressed Irish industry.
While the matter was in progress, Irish
affairs occupied a large share of attention in
the newspapers; and here also Macpherson was
specially employed in presenting the case of
the Government in a favourable light to the
public.   Facts and arguments were, it appears,
sometimes supplied to him by the executive.
The following letter, addressed to John Robinson, then patronage secretary to the Treasury,
shows the light in which Macpherson was at
this time regarded by the Government, and
the nature of the services which he performed.
It is further interesting from the evidence
which it affords that Macpherson was now
casting about for a seat in the House of Commons.

" Private.

" Dear Sir,

" Though, I suppose, Irish affairs are so well settled that they will not require any discussion before the public, I wish to have my notes ; and, if convenient, the copy of the accounts furnished by the Custom Houses on both sides of the water. These last I shall return, whenever they may be wanted. I shall call for both when you are at leisure to point them out.

" I left to-day, in Parliament Street, two letters for Lord North, which came enclosed to me from Quebec.

" You may perhaps recollect that last year I made some efforts to obtain a seat in a certain place, at the particular injunctions of a friend. I shall now defer any attempts of the same kind to the general election, unless the remainder of the present P——t could be prefixed to the ensuing year. I am armed with powers for both. . . . May I request you turning this subject in your mind at a leisure hour? The pointing out the line is all that is wanted, as the affair will be managed, without any interference. A particular friend is also on the same scent. I know that such things could be obtained for both, did we once know how and where the ground lies.

" I am, with much esteem and regard,
" Dear Sir,
" Your most obedient humble servant,
" J. M.[1]

" December 18, 1779."

[1] The Marquess of Abergavenny's MSS. at Eridge. The remaining letters to John Robinson are from the same source.

The first friend here mentioned was not improbably John Macpherson, who in the previous April had been elected for Cricklade, and was now pressing the nabob's claims upon Parliament. He had no difficulty in inducing his friends to give him their support. For the office was not without its attractions : there was something reputable in attacking the Company, and something lucrative in the rewards of the nabob; and it is hardly surprising to find that at this time there were no less than six members of the House under the suspicion of receiving money from Arcot. During his stay at home, John Macpherson had risen in the estimation of ministers, and he was now about to return to India as a member of the Supreme Council. The appointment, it is true, met with severe criticism, on the ground that the support which he had given to a native prince had endangered the peace of India ; but he retained his seat, and eventually succeeded Warren Hastings as Governor-General. On leaving for India he induced the nabob to allow Macpherson to be his agent in London,[1] and Macpherson, it appears, was eager to accept the post. He was now

---

[1] Wraxall's *Memoirs*, ed. Wheatley, iv. 83.

known to take a strong interest in Indian affairs. The elder of the Sulivans mentioned in the next letter, which is also addressed to Robinson, had been in the service of the nabob, and was now an official of the Company.[1]

"Private.

"Dear Sir,

"I am exceedingly obliged by the letter to the nabob mentioning my friend, young Mr. Sulivan. It seems that he told old Mr. Sulivan of this piece of your politeness, who seems to be much struck with it; for he called upon me last night to signify his extreme anxiety to co-operate with you, in proper measures, at the present crisis of the Company's affairs. . . . He is very much displeased with the present propositions, as very inadequate to what the public ought to derive from a whole Empire, which Providence has thrown in the way, as it were, to save the nation in its finance-distress.

"He informs me that it is his fixed opinion that the proprietors, under the proposed terms, will never have more than their present dividend; and he says he can stake his reputation upon it, that Government will never get a shilling, if these propositions are to be the foundation of the new charter. He insinuated that the best thing possible that could happen is that the proposals should be rejected by the wild orators of Leadenhall Street, which he believes and even hopes will be the case. He says it is impossible to conceive how much those who understand the

[1] The Eridge MSS.

subject, and who are friends of the State, are disappointed; and he thinks that even many who will publicly avow the contrary will desert the directors on a ballot, and join even with the mad party to defeat the propositions.

" He told me the particulars relative to the advances made to him by the Attorney-General, and that his chief reason for evading them was his determination to fight under no banner without your concurrence. In short, he expresses so much anxiety to be well with Government, and of co-operating entirely with you, and you only, that I cannot have the least doubt of his present sincerity, or the future rectitude of his conduct. He says that he has, as much as possible, avoided even to listen to some in Leadenhall Street who wished to make a stalking horse of him against the Government, always wishing and expecting that Government would call him forward to facilitate these views.

" He, however, observed that the partially taking him up, and not supporting him, would only throw disgrace on his old age and make him obnoxious to friends whom he can otherwise easily lead. The purport of the whole was, that he wished his sentiments to be conveyed by some proper and secret means to you, with the most solemn engagements on his part, that he will, if supported, himself support Government with the utmost zeal and fidelity, and he trusts with great success.

" Though there is no office I understand less or dislike more than that of mediator, I could not refuse to write to you on the subject. My sincere opinion is, that you will find Mr. S. extremely useful and direct. He knows the management of the directors and the business of the Company much better than any man in the India House, and, what is more, he will be a very effectual check on those men who, I know, will endeavour to carry the influence of the Company to the Admiralty and Lincoln's Inn.

" I request the favour that you will consider this subject and burn this letter. I wish to have some answer to give to the old man, who, I suppose, will consider even my silence as a kind of refusal of his request.

" I am, with great sincerity and esteem,
" Dear Sir,
" Your most faithful humble servant,

" JAMES MACPHERSON.
" London, 5th Feb., 1780."

The intervention was successful ; for by the end of April Sulivan was chairman of the committee of correspondence. Sulivan's later conduct, when he became chairman of the Company, was not such as to escape the strongest censure by the Select Committee appointed to examine into the Company's affairs.

Macpherson's desire for a seat in the House was soon gratified ; as in the general election of 1780 he was returned for one of the Cornish boroughs, at that time usually in the nomination of the Government. On 11th September, he became junior member for Camelford. At the famous election in April, 1784, when the younger

Pitt swept the country, Macpherson became senior member, and he retained the seat for the rest of his life.[1]   Of his activity in Parliament little is known.   He never attempted to address the House ; but his services were useful to Government, and he received a secret pension of £500.[2] His conduct of the newspapers after he entered Parliament began to excite the anger of the Whigs, and their anger was to some extent a measure of the importance of the part which Macpherson was now playing.[3]

His own affairs received no small share of attention ; and in the convulsions which followed Fox's East India Bill he became aware of many secrets which he put to his private use by

---

[1] *Return of Members of Parliament.*

[2] His name is included in a confidential list of parliamentary pensioners among Robinson's papers in the Eridge MSS.

[3] See Walpole's *Letters*, viii. 186.   Walpole, writing in March, 1782, speaks of the ministerial crisis : "The Erse nation is furious at Lord North.   Fingal himself told him : ' Remember, my Lord, I do not desert you '.   And again : ' Most things are in the newspapers now as soon as they happen, and so are ten thousand things that don't happen. . . . Who can winnow them but on the spot ?   I pity posterity, who will not be able to discern one thousandth part of the lies of Macpherson and Bate.' "

speculating with success. In this he was following the example of many other supporters
of the Ministry, who made great fortunes at
this time. From 1783 onwards he held his
office of agent to the nabob in conjunction
with Sir Nathaniel Wraxall. He removed
from Manchester Buildings to Norfolk Street,
Strand; and a private coach of some splendour carried him to and fro between his house
in town and his villa at Putney.

The following letter, which is undated, has
been preserved; it was addressed to Woodfall,
the well-known publisher, who was on terms
of intimacy with Macpherson, and, as the
letter appears to indicate, was sometimes employed by him in confidential business. There
is some reason to suppose that it belongs
to this period. For "Old Paul," of whom
he speaks, is probably Paul Benfield, notorious
from a vehement attack made upon him by
Burke. He was accused of dishonesty and
disloyalty ; but although his character does
not appear to have been estimable, it is fair
to his memory, and to Macpherson, to record
that the specific charges that were brought
against him were disproved.

King's head Ivey-Lane
5 o' clock. July 21.

Dear Sir

I wandered into this house to take a solitary chop, Hoping that you were not otherwise engaged, I sent to your house, to request your company to a bottle of Wine. I have several scraps of intelligence, for Old Paul, but, what with Porter and beef steaks, I am so indolent or so stupid, that I cannot commit them to paper, without the aid of an Amanuensis. If your other engagements will permit you to look in upon me, within an hour, you will find me and do me a favour. If not will you and your brother favour me, at Putney, on Satur: day next, to dinner? Will your brother carry mrs Woodfall? Poor Becket is to come and bring his daughter under his wing; and I seriously wish to have two, rather than one woman. Let him come cum Sequela. I have room and Welcome for you all.

Yours affectionately
James Macpherson.

While Macpherson was immersed in political and financial speculations, two of his friends in Edinburgh were bearing the brunt of the Ossianic controversy, which had now passed from argu-

ment to sheer abuse. A sentence in Shaw's
Inquiry proclaimed to the world that Blair and
Ferguson had practised a base deception on
Bishop Percy, in that, while he was in Edinburgh in the year 1763, some pieces of old
Gaelic had been recited to him as the original
of certain passages in *Fingal.* In the preface to
the first edition of the *Reliques of Ancient Poetry*,
this fact was alleged as definite proof that the
work was authentic; but in the second and
third editions of the *Reliques* the allegation was
omitted. It was against Ferguson that the
charge was chiefly directed; and he took it up
with great warmth. A long correspondence
ensued. That Gaelic poems of some sort had
been brought to Percy's notice was on neither
side denied; but as the facts in dispute had
happened some eighteen years previously, there
was little chance of any agreement.[1]

[1] The reader will find some of the letters in Small's
Biog. Sketch of Adam Ferguson. In the Egerton MSS. in
the British Museum there is a letter from Ferguson to
Bishop Douglas, dated Edinburgh, 21st July, 1781, in which
he declared that everything that related to him in Shaw's
pamphlet was false, and that he never was present at any
repetition of verses to Percy, although he remembers showing
him some scraps of Earse poetry. He proceeded to attack

At the same time Macpherson's friends were
anxious that he should withdraw his attention
from public affairs, and bring out the originals
himself. But his friends were mostly satisfied
as to the authenticity of his work ; and the successful Scotchman was hardly the man to relax
his political activity or diminish his fortune
for the sake of satisfying abusive opponents.
Sir John Sinclair tells us that about this period
he was frequently in Macpherson's company,
both in London and at Putney, and that he took
various opportunities of urging him to complete
the publication, and that, in spite of certain
efforts, nothing effectual was accomplished.
But in 1783 there came an appeal which could
not ultimately be resisted. In response to a
circular by Sir John Macgregor Murray, some

the obstinate incredulity of the critics. " These gentlemen,
I see, are never to be convinced : if conjectural evidence is
brought, they call out for direct testimony ; if testimony,
they call out for the Ipsa corpora. If the Ipsa corpora,
then Mr. Macpherson or some one else has made a translation
into Earse from the original English of Mr. Macpherson's
forgery. . . . If there be no merit in these productions they
ought to have been forgotten long ago. The specimens I
have seen are very interesting . . . and whether genuine
or spurious, I shall never be ashamed of having mistaken
them for originals."

Highland gentlemen in the Company's service in India collected a sum of nearly a thousand pounds, and sent it to the Highland Society of London, together with a high-flown letter to Macpherson, entreating him to gratify the wishes of his countrymen. John Mackenzie, secretary to the society, and an intimate friend, forwarded the money to Macpherson, and asked him to receive a formal deputation. To this Macpherson made the following reply :—

"Norfolk Street, 4th July, 1784.
"My dear Sir,
"I received the favour of your letter, dated yesterday ; and I am sorry the gentlemen should think of giving themselves the trouble of waiting upon me, as a ceremony of that kind is altogether superfluous and unnecessary. I shall adhere to the promise I made several years ago to a deputation of the same kind ; that is, to employ my first leisure time, and a considerable portion of time it *must* be to do it accurately, in arranging and printing the originals of the *Poems of Ossian*, as they have come to my hands. Funds having been established for the expense, there can be no excuse, but want of leisure, for not commencing the work in a very few months.
"I am, with my best respects to the gentlemen of the committee,
"My dear Sir,
"Your faithful humble servant,
"JAMES MACPHERSON.
"John Mackenzie, Esq., etc."

[1] Sinclair, *op. cit.*, i. ccxx.

Nevertheless, a few weeks later, a deputation sought and obtained an interview with Macpherson, when; as appears by the minutes of the society, he expressed his sense of the great honour done him, and repeated his intention to publish the original Gaelic of Ossian with his first leisure.

The period of leisure had not yet arrived, and for some years further nothing was done. Macpherson was at the height of his social career in London. The Government was grateful enough for his services to make him an offer of the estates of Cluny Macpherson, which had been confiscated for nearly forty years; but he was strictly loyal to his clan, and the estates passed to their rightful owner.[1] In 1785 he was received by the Prince of Wales, who presented him with a token of his regard. And in the same year, on the death of Whitehead, we find Macpherson's name in the long list of candidates for the office of poet laureate.[2]

---

[1] Carruthers, *loc. cit.*

[2] Thomas Warton was elected. One of the newspapers of the day in a tone of parody described an imaginary poetical combat between the candidates. A writer in the *Celtic Magazine* quotes the poem assigned to Macpherson as a serious and original effort.

CHAPTER XIII.

MACPHERSON'S LATER LIFE IN BADENOCH.—JOINS
THE WHIGS.—THE DEBATES ON THE REGENCY
BILL.—LETTERS TO ROBINSON.—THE GAELIC
ORIGINALS.—MACPHERSON'S CHILDREN.—HIS
LAST DAYS.

WHILE Macpherson was still in the prime of life
and in the full tide of success, he prepared to
spend the evening of his days amongst his own
people. If he had cherished any ambition of
making a figure in the world, the ambition had
long been satisfied ; and his thoughts turned
again to Badenoch. There he resolved to invest
some of his fortune in buying land, and in building a house within sight of his native hills.

He formed an estate on the banks of the
Spey by taking over two or three small pro-
perties. Of these the principal lay to the east
of the valley of Kingussie and not far from Loch
Inch. It had formerly been the seat of Mackintosh of Borlum, who had disgraced his clan
by a system of bare robbery on the highway,
instead of contenting himself with levying black-

mail, after the legitimate practice of the times; and, as the very name of his house had become notorious, Macpherson changed it to Belleville. Adam, the most conspicuous architect of the day, was engaged to design in its place a handsome villa in the Italian style.

Macpherson spent his money freely, and in the circle of his neighbours he had a reputation for kindness and generosity. In building his house he was careful to employ none but native workmen; and to these he paid, for a day's work, half as much again as they usually received. It was his wish, he declared, to make every poor Highlander on his estate a comfortable and happy man.[1] Nor was he, after the fashion of some successful persons, forgetful of those who had helped him in his own time of need. In his early struggles as a poor schoolmaster in Ruthven, a farmer in the neighbourhood had more than once given him money. The farmer had now become his tenant; and when he came to pay his rent, Macpherson, we learn, received him with conspicuous courtesy, and of his own accord desired him, out of the pasture-land on the estate, to select and enclose as much as he

[1] Carruthers, *loc. cit.*

thought proper for a maintenance. Of this he offered him unconditionally a freehold for life.[1]

Of Macpherson's doings whenever he retired to Belleville some slight record was preserved by his friend Mrs. Ann Grant of Laggan in her well-known *Letters from the Mountains.* This remarkable lady was very pleased to have him for a neighbour, in spite of the pious horror with which she heard of some of his adventures. In October, 1788, she indulged her poetical fancies over the Highlander's return to his own country.

"The bard of bards, who reached the mouldy harp of Ossian from the withered oak of Selma, and awakened the song of other times, is now moving, like a bright meteor, over his native hills; and while the music of departed bards awakes the joy of grief, the spirits of departed warriors lean from their bright clouds to hear. . . . The bard, as I was about to tell you, is as great a favourite of fortune as of fame, and has got more by the old harp of Ossian than most of his predecessors could draw out of the silver strings of Apollo. He has bought three small estates in this country within the last two years, given a ball to young ladies, and made other exhibitions of wealth and liberality. He now keeps a hall at Belleville, his new purchased

[1] See the preface to the Rev. P. Hately Waddell's *Ossian, Historical and Authentic.* The story was told by a living representative of the person to whom the offer was made.

seat, where there are as many shells as are in Selma, filled, I doubt not, with much better liquor."[1]

When he was settled in his house, he lived, according to the same informant, "with all the state and hospitality of a chieftain". Carruthers[2] tells of his cheerful habits.

"After a forenoon's writing, he used to mount his horse, sally out and bring home with him troops of friends from both sides of the Spey. Then with wine and jest—and no man was more various and fascinating in society —the festivities were prolonged far into the night."

But it was only during a few months in the summer and autumn that Macpherson could entertain his Highland friends at Belleville; the business of the nabob and parliamentary duties still compelled him to spend most of the year in London. Although his health began to give him trouble, he had still sufficient energy to follow the political intrigues of the lobby, and play his small part behind the scenes.

His kinsman, Sir John, had now joined the Whig opposition, partly, it appears, out of a desire to stand well with the Prince of Wales;

[1] ii. 133.   [2] *Op. cit.*

and there are indications in the remainder of the letters to Robinson that Macpherson followed the same course, probably for the same reason. He was pleased with the change. " My new friends," he wrote, "are in one respect not like the old ; they don't harass me with cards, or call people to nothing."[1] Of his activity in the House during the debates on the Regency Bill, when he was following the course of the great combat between Pitt and Fox, some record has been preserved.

The events which led up to that measure are matters of familiar history. Towards the end of 1788 the King's insanity had become so marked that it was no longer possible to keep it from the public ; but the unpopularity of the Prince, and his open sympathy with the Opposition, made the question of the Regency one of great embarrassment to Pitt and the Government. In December the physicians in attendance on the King had certified that he was for the present totally incapacitated for taking any part in public business. Fox declared that the Prince had an inherent right to assume the reins of Government ; but Pitt, maintaining that

[1] The Eridge MSS.

it was the business of Parliament to settle the
question, moved and carried his resolution that
the Prince should be invested with the royal
authority subject to certain limitations on his
power.   In order to overcome a constitutional
difficulty, it was further proposed that the great
seal as the formal expression of the royal assent
should be put in commission, and that the two
Houses of Parliament should authorise the
commission to affix the royal assent to the Bill
creating the Regency.   On 6th January, the day
on which Pitt had intended to introduce the
limitations, the Opposition successfully objected
that, as a month had elapsed since the physicians'
report, a fresh examination should take place
before any decision was taken.   Macpherson
was in active correspondence with Robinson.
On the 9th he wrote to tell him of the eagerness with which the committee's report was
expected, the annoyance at the delay, and the
rumours of dissension ; and he kept him well
informed of the course of events.

" London, 24th Jan., 1789.

   " My dear Sir,

      " I received the favour of your letter, and
I am exceedingly sorry for your indisposition.

I have been so much employed in some private
affairs for these several days past, that it was
impossible for me to go, as I wished, to Syon
Hill. Your hints were conveyed, and were well
received. Nothing new of a private nature. I
suppose the Lords finished their part of the
business last night, and consequently that on
Monday they will return the resolutions to the
Lower House. Tuesday, therefore, will be the
great day. If anything material occurs inter-
medially, you will hear from me. I wish you a
speedy recovery ; and I ever am,

"Very faithfully yours,

"J. MACPHERSON."

"26th Jan., 1789.

"I am just returned from the House. The
conference was held ; the resolutions returned,
as agreed to. Mr. Pitt moved to adjourn till
to-morrow ; when he is to bring forward a resolution to send a message from the House, or
rather Houses, to the Prince, to inform him of
what has been done, and to know whether he will
accept the government on the terms proposed.
. . . I do not find the *Seal Scheme* is given up,
so that I see no short end to this same settle-
ment. This week will be taken up by the
Message. The next will probably be too little
for the Seal ; and God knows how much time
the Bill itself will require. I believe all this is
done to give time for addresses. I am much
hurried, the bellman being at the door. The P.
is much pleased with the communication sent.

"J. M.

"Monday, 6 o'clock."

"29th Jan., 1789.

" My dear Sir,

"I write this in much haste : the bellman at the door. We have adjourned to Monday, 70 to 51. The Lords go upon the Seal business on Saturday. The Prince is to give his answer to-morrow at *three.* There are apprehensions of B——ke's being in the Board of Controul. He insists upon it for the services and utterance of *thirty years.* If they will agree, all the fat will be in the fire. A hint to the P. would prevent it, for I plainly see his object is to carry on business as smoothly as he can. But how to give the hint is the question. They have carried the question against Mr. Pitt in the Common Council to-day. I wish much to see you on various matters. I am told the answer is guarded—but decisive. *His own* ideas. He has written a very proper letter—an ostensible one, should the K. recover, to the Q. That also his own.

"Yours most faithfully,

"J. M."

From time to time Macpherson bethought himself of the promise which he had given to the Highland Society, that he would use his first leisure to arrange and print the Gaelic originals of *Ossian.* It remains to show that what was meant by an arrangement of the originals was a process of bringing them into a greater agreement with the English version than in fact existed.

They were, as we know, for the most part fragments taken down from oral recitation. The
business in hand was not only to reduce them
to the same order as had been followed in the
English version, and to supply a Gaelic text for
so much of that version as had been formed by
interpolations and amendments, but also, in the
uncouth state of the language, to devise some
definite scheme of Gaelic orthography. Macpherson's transcripts had been rough and hurried,
and in parts, it will be remembered, so mechanical
that he and his friends had disputed as to the
meaning of words and phrases, and had been compelled, in some cases where the language was un-
intelligible, to substitute passages agreeing with
the spirit of the context. Moreover, the transcripts were now thirty years old and long
neglected. In the work which Macpherson was
called upon to do for the Highland Society he
had the assistance of Mackenzie himself, and
also of Captain Morison, who was employed to
copy out the poems.[1] That the work was in a
large measure linguistic is sufficiently apparent
from a letter to Morison in August, 1789.
Macpherson was making an attempt to treat

[1] Sinclair, *op. cit.*, i. lxxxix.

19

Gaelic in a scientific fashion all his own. "Not only *Ossian*," he wrote, "but much more is going on; the establishing the whole language on primitive, clear, unerring and incontrovertible principles. The Gaelic, now traced to its source, has already been found to be the most regular, the most simple, the most pleasing to the ear, ·and *almost* to the eye, of any language either of past or present times." [1]

In the matter of the originals Mackenzie was, it seems, completely in Macpherson's confidence, and the two friends made some definite arrangement in regard to their publication. This fact is clearly established. Macpherson expressly provided in his will that the sum of money sent from India was to be left to Mackenzie for the purpose of defraying the expense of printing the originals on a plan concerted between them,[2] if that publication should not have taken place before his own death. Amongst his books and papers a copy of the first edition of the poems was discovered, with notes and memoranda affixed to some of them in his own handwriting,

[1] Graham's *Essay on the Authenticity of Ossian*, App., p. 445.

[2] See the copy of his will in Somerset House.

by which it appears that he had delivered the whole or parts of their originals to Mackenzie.[1] Nor is this all; for an entry in Mackenzie's diary, in which he was in the habit of noting any important events, has been preserved, showing on what terms he stood with Macpherson. The secretary to the Highland Society could hardly, perhaps, have been deceived where Gaelic language or literature was concerned; but it cannot be doubted that some at least of the fragments which he saw required a great amount of elaboration before they could be presented to the public.

"22nd July.—Went at one o'clock to Putney Common, to Mr. Macpherson. He said he had been searching in an old trunk upstairs, which he had with him in East Florida, for the original of *Berrathon*. That he feared it was in an imperfect condition, and that part of it was wanting, as of *Carthon;* that he had only put together a few lines of it, and those not to his own liking; that he had tired of it after a short sitting.

"He took notice of the fine simile, which is a separate fragment, and not a part of any poem, which is in my possession, where he thinks there is a proof contained of the existence of the aurora borealis in the days of Ossian. In fact, however, the simile contains no such proof. I concluded from thence, that the simile was not

[1] *Rep.*, pp. 32, 33.

of his composition, because he would hardly
introduce in it a striking circumstance that
every one knows could not apply to those early
times ; as every one knows the aurora borealis
has appeared in the sky in latter times only.[1]

"I made the same conclusion from his ascribing the same striking circumstance to the simile,
which circumstance does in fact exist in it.   Mr.
Macpherson has on several occasions in the most
off-hand manner, in the course of conversation,
thought the knowledge of navigation among the
Gael in those early days was evidently proved
by the names they had given to certain stars, as
appear in a poem of Temora.

"Came to town in Mr. Macpherson's carriage
in the evening."[2]

It was a conceit of Macpherson's that he
might avoid all the intricacies of Gaelic orthography, and render the language in its pris-
tine form, if he used Greek characters.   This
idea he drew from a statement made by
Cæsar that the Druids used them.[3]   He had,

[1] This, of course, was a very erroneous assumption on
Mackenzie's part ; for if it is the case that there is no
mention of an aurora in ancient literature, it is because that
literature comes from countries where even a faint aurora
is a very rare occurrence.   If Macpherson was right in his
notion, it is a curious piece of evidence.

[2] Sinclair, *op. cit.*, i. xc.

[3] Cf. *De Bello Gallico*, i. 29 : "In castris Helvetiorum
tabulæ reportæ sunt litteris Græcis confectæ".   Cf. also vi.,
14, 15.

of course, no difficulty in showing that the existing method of writing and speaking Gaelic was unsatisfactory, as could not fail to be the case when the same letter represented different sounds, and similar sounds were expressed by different letters; and, again, when many words contained letters that were never pronounced. He did not, as far as can now be determined, explain how the use of Greek characters would obviate these linguistic embarrassments, or more accurately reflect the niceties of Gaelic pronunciation; but, by way of experiment, he had a passage from the Gaelic Bible printed in Gaelic and in Greek characters side by side. He then endeavoured to argue his friends into an acceptance of his scheme. The following letter, addressed to Adam Ferguson, at that time in Edinburgh, shows that Macpherson had a very strong opinion on the matter.

" London, 21st May, 1793.

" My dear Sir,

" I wrote you a few lines some time ago, wherein, if I recollect aright, I promised to send me soon after an answer to your letter of the 8th of April on the subject of the proposed printing of the original of the *Poems of Ossian* in the Greek

character. Having been, at the time of receiving your letter, immersed in a hurry of business,
from which I have not as yet wholly extricated
myself, I desired a gentleman, who has for
many years in conjunction with myself thought
critically of the Gaelic language, to throw our
opinion upon paper, at his convenience, more for
your satisfaction than from either a wish or expectation of making converts of others. This he has
done accordingly, as you will find under another
cover, which goes by to-morrow's post. As my
friend has left little that is material for me to
add, I shall not trouble you with a long letter.

"Our friend, Dr. Blair, I perceive, labours
under much want of information on the subject;
for there is not one of the points on which he
states his objections founded in fact; and, that
being the case, his arguments and reasons require no answer. I cannot conceive what interest, except it was a silly degree of vanity, to
give themselves a consequence on account of
their knowledge in the Gaelic, those persons
who gave the information had in deceiving our
friend.

"Mr. Davidson writes rationally, but he seems
not to know that there is scarce any manuscript
to be followed, except, indeed, a very few mutilated ones in a kind of Saxon characters, which
was utterly unknown to the Highlanders as
either the Greek or Hebrew letters. With respect to the cheap copy he mentions, if there
should arise a wish for having a small edition,
there is scarce any common printer but can
metamorphose the Greek character into something like it in the Roman. With respect to the
splendid edition now intended, it was never my
intention to put it up to sale, so that its grandeur

will not keep it out of the hands of those who would enjoy it most. I believe it will appear, from the accompanying observations, that there are not many of those amateurs between Glotta and Tarvisium. . . .

"As I have heard that Mr. Davidson is an excellent Greek scholar, he may be induced, perhaps, to try the effect of the specimen now sent on the Highland porter, or chairman, in the manner recommended in the accompanying observations. Our friend Mr. Home and even Dr. Blair, who are both good Grecians, will be able, I trust, to read the original of *Ossian*, as it is to be printed in Greek, in a manner that will be intelligible to such Highlanders as understand their native tongue. But these, I apprehend, are much more circumscribed in number than is generally supposed.

"The result of the whole is that I have resolved to follow the example of the old Druids, in writing the Celtic language in Greek characters. I shall not therefore, with Dr. Blair, agree 'that it is the opinion of some of the *learned* in *Earse* that must determine the point, and that to them it *must be submitted*'. Where these learned men are, I have never been able to learn. With respect to the clergy, I would rather take their ghostly advice on matters of religion than accept of their opinion about the manner of printing profane poetry. I consequently request, that instead of submitting the decision to them, you will be pleased to return to me the specimen, already in your hands, at your convenience. And after having weighed the observations, at your full leisure, and at your own time, you will please to put them also under a cover to me. You will easily perceive that this letter is meant only for your own eye ; for few men wish to know that they have so long deceived, on a point which the smallest attention might at once ascertain.   With my best respects to all friends,

" I am, with great esteem,

" Yours most faithfully,

" JAMES MACPHERSON." [1]

Although Ferguson replied to this letter in a tone of general approval, Macpherson received no encouragement from other friends.   Blair, at whom the concluding remarks were obviously aimed, gave himself, it seems, the greatest pains to discredit the proposal as a piece of sheer affectation ; and soon afterwards it was finally abandoned.   Macpherson still hesitated to send any part of the originals to the press; and he continued to hesitate until death overtook him.

In his furious letter Johnson had spoken of Macpherson's morals, as though their colour affected the arguments in the controversy.   The truth of the matter is, that, like many greater and more distinguished men in those and other times, Macpherson had various adventures of a kind which is not generally recorded in bio-

---

[1] MSS. University of Edinburgh, quoted in Small's *Biog. Sketch of Adam Ferguson*, p. 53.

graphies. He was the father of five children.[1]
To give the names of their mothers would now
serve no useful purpose whatever ; but it is to
be set down to his credit that, unlike some more
distinguished men, he made ample provision for
all his children, and settled on their several
mothers a comfortable annuity. By the irony
of life, this very mark of constancy exposed
him to the contempt of domesticated friends ;
and Mrs. Grant bewailed the fact that, like
other bachelors, he had become " the dupe
of wretched toad-eaters and designing house-
keepers ".

His letters to Robinson show that whether
he was in London or in Badenoch, he had to
the close of his life no lack of business for the
nabob.

[1] See the copy of his will. There were three sons and
two daughters. Of the sons, the eldest, James, became
before his father's death a lieutenant in the East India
Company's service, and he succeeded to the estates ; the
second, Charles, educated at Hampstead, died early in
India ; of the third, born in 1783, the name is not known.
His daughters were Ann, who succeeded James in the estates,
and died childless ; and Juliet, who was brought up in a
boarding school at Putney. In 1810 Juliet married Mr.,
afterwards Sir David Brewster ; and his descendants took
the name Macpherson.

"Belleville, 24th Oct., 1794.

" Private.

"In the end of September I set out on my annual excursion to this place, where I have been for almost these four weeks past. One is so bewildered by the assertions of news writers that it is difficult to form any judgment of what is passing. In several of these *faithful* vehicles of intelligence, it is said that Parliament is soon to be dissolved. On this subject, I solicit to hear from you, as soon as may be convenient, addressing to me at this place, by Inverness, N.B. I have desired my friend Mr. Duncan to wait upon you on *another matter*, to explain things that would swell this letter to too large a size. Whatever opinion or advice you may be pleased to give will be communicated to me by Mr. Duncan. This country is very quiet, and I believe perfectly loyal. The season has been good, and plenty establishes content. It will depend on circumstances whether or not I shall be in town at the meeting of the House. But at any rate I shall, health serving, be there before Christmas."

"Putney Heath, 5th April, 1795.

"I intended to step over to Syon Hill this forenoon, but the uncertainty of finding you at leisure, the gloomy aspect of the day, and it being so unseasonably cold, prevents it. In consequence of my letter, I expected for these ten days past to have heard from you with the letters and memorandum relative to Mr. Myers. I should suppose we are now too late for the first batch of India ships; for it was only *supposed*, that a packet which I sent yesterday from the India House, would overtake the *Lord Thurlow* at Portsmouth, the wind being good and favourable for conveying her round from the Downs.

"I have had a letter from the N. of the 29th of September last. He had received all my letters by the India fleet which sailed in May, as per a signed list, which was returned to me enclosed. The new government had taken the reins and began to act; and, in the usual way with all Madras-successions, had offered a new treaty. In consequence of the advice given, the proposal was resisted and refused.

"I have enclosed herein our case in the House of Lords. . . . I should suppose the Princess Elect is by this time arrived. The mob crowded the streets last evening in the hope of her coming."

"Putney Common, 15th June, 1795.

"I have been busy for more than a week past in writing by the Indiamen that had got round to Portsmouth; otherwise I should have taken my chance of finding you disengaged at Syon Hill, for a few minutes. The ships, after having been ordered to sail and not to sail, alternately for several times, are now, I am told, by favour of a north-east wind, out of reach of our versatile councils.

"The East India Company have at length come forward with their Case, of which I enclose a copy for your perusal at your leisure. I shall make no comment upon it, leaving it entirely to your better judgment."

There is little more to be told. In the autumn of 1795 Macpherson was late in leaving

London; in September he was still at Putney, writing to Robinson on the business of the East India fleet. When he arrived in the Highlands, he determined, contrary to his custom, to remain there for the winter. He dallied with his Gaelic originals; and in spite of broken health, he continued to entertain his friends, and to assist the poor. In these occupations his life came to its end.

Of his last days Mrs. Grant has preserved a brief record, interspersed with her own reflections on his character.

" He was a very good-natured man; and now that he had got all his schemes of interest and ambition fulfilled, he seemed to reflect and grow domestic, and showed of late a great inclination to be an indulgent landlord and very liberal to the poor; of which I could relate various instances more tender and interesting than flashy and ostentatious. His heart and temper were originally good. His religious principles were, I fear, unfixed and fluctuating; but the primary cause that so much genius, taste, benevolence, and prosperity did not produce or diffuse more happiness, was his living a stranger to the comforts of domestic life, from which unhappy connections excluded him."

Macpherson died on February 17, 1796.

"On Friday last C. V. R. dined there. James had been indisposed since the great storm; yet received his guests with much kindness, seeming, however, languid and dispirited. Towards evening he sank much and retired early. Next morning he appeared, but did not eat, and looked ill. R. begged he would frank a cover for Charlotte; he did so, and never more held a pen. When they left the house, he was taken extremely ill, unable to move or receive nourishment, though perfectly sensible. Before this attack, finding some inward symptoms of his approaching dissolution, he sent for a consultation, the result of which arrived the day after his confinement. He was perfectly sensible and collected, yet refused to take anything prescribed to him to the last; and that, on this principle, that his time was come, and it did not avail. He felt the approaches of death, and hoped no relief from medicine; though his life was not such as one should like to look back on at that awful period,—indeed, whose is? It pleased the Almighty to render his last scene most affecting and exemplary. He died last Tuesday evening; and from the minute he was confined to a very little before he expired, never ceased imploring the Divine mercy in the most earnest and pathetic manner."

In his will Macpherson left a sum of money for the erection of a monument on his own land, and in a codicil he directed, after a practice permissible at the time, that his remains should be carried in the most decent manner from Scotland to the Abbey of Westminster; for that, he wrote, was "the city wherein I lived and passed the greatest and best part of my life".

His body was brought to London.   At High-gate, after being eighteen days on the road, it was met by many of his friends, and a long row of carriages followed it to the Abbey.[1]   On 15th March it was buried in the south transept, not far from Poets' Corner.   A plain inscription marks the grave.

[1] *Gentleman's Magazine*, 1796, p. 256.

CHAPTER XIV.

SUBSEQUENT HISTORY OF THE POEMS.—LAING'S
ATTACK.—SCOTT.—THE HIGHLAND SOCIETY'S
REPORT.—PUBLICATION OF THE ORIGINALS.—
FURTHER CONTROVERSY.—CONCLUSION.

IT remains to sketch the history and fate of the
question which Macpherson left as a legacy to
friends and enemies alike.

Having slumbered for fifteen years, the controversy broke out afresh on his death. In 1797
the Highland Society of Scotland appointed a
committee to collect what material or information it was still practicable to collect, regarding
the nature of the poems ascribed to Ossian, and
particularly of those published by Macpherson;
but not, as it was expressly agreed, to enter
into any elaborate arguments on their authenticity or to examine conflicting theories. The
committee consisted of some of the best Celtic
scholars of Scotland, and its chairman was
Henry Mackenzie.

While the committee was engaged in its
labours the authenticity of the poems was

fiercely attacked by Malcolm Laing, a writer of much zeal and industry, who marshalled great stores of historical knowledge with the skill and vigour of a practised advocate. Some of his criticism has already been noticed. In an Appendix to his *History of Scotland*,[1] published in Edinburgh in 1800, he denounced the whole of the poems as a mere patchwork of plagiarism from a hundred sources ancient and modern. Five years later he published the poems in an edition of his own, in which he examined them line for line for the purpose of making good his charge ; and he professed to find nearly a thousand instances of plagiarism from eighty-eight authors. Laing's criticism over-reached and confuted itself. It has been shown[2] that whereas he spent some eight or ten years of mature life in making this astonishing collection, with leisure, wealth, ease, friends to help him, and all the resources of the Advocates' Library at his command, Macpherson, poor and young, did the whole of his work in a short time, and before he was twenty-six. To give an increased

---

[1] Vol. ii. p. 377.

[2] By Dr. Hately Waddell, *op. cit.*, who gives a formidable list of the alleged quotations and of the authors from whom they were supposed to be drawn.

importance to the poems, Macpherson, probably assisted by Blair, had pointed out over a hundred passages which bore a resemblance to parts of the Bible, Homer, Milton, and so on ; and in rendering them it is not unlikely that he was anxious to increase the resemblance both in thought and in style ; much, indeed, as Pope admittedly used the style of Milton in order to give dignity and grace to his own version of Homer.[1] Of the similarities on which Laing put his finger, the larger number shows a mere verbal parallel, in most cases very slight, and not beyond the limits of chance. It is impossible to believe that if the Ossianic poems had been fashioned by such wholesale robbery, they could have had merit or character enough to influence the literature of Europe. Laing's chief fault was that he overlooked the simple probabilities of the case. It is most unlikely, from the character of all Macpherson's other publications, that he could be the sole author of the poems, or that he could have written their twenty thousand lines in so brief a period.

But Laing went beyond the charge of plagiarism. He cited two alleged admissions made by

[1] See Pope's postscript to his translation of the *Odyssey*.

Macpherson,[1] that he had himself written the
work.   But the evidence by which he sought
to establish these admissions was of a character
ridiculously slight.   A Dr. Anderson had, he
said, declared that Bishop Percy had been posi-
tively assured by Sir John Eliot that a certain
statement had been made to him by Macpherson; and again, a Highland minister had maintained that he had been told by a General
Plunket that a friend of his had received from
Macpherson a similar assurance.   No one can
place much credence in what A declares that
B had mentioned as having told him by C
about some admission by D.   Macpherson had
a large number of intimate friends; and in the
thirty years of his life in London he must, by
all accounts, often have been in the condition
in which a man is apt to disclose secrets.   He
was pleased to mystify the public; but if he had
written the poems he could hardly have failed
sometimes to reveal the fact to his friends.

As additional evidence of their spurious
nature, Laing mentioned the introduction of
rhyme into Ossian before it was known in

---

[1] Laing, *op. cit.*, i. xx.; see also Nicholls' *Lit. Illustr.*, viii.
417.

Europe, and the identification of the Balclutha of Ossian with the Alcuith of Bede. He endeavoured to show, further, that the real authorship of the poems was placed beyond dispute by the use of biblical phrases, as Macpherson at the time of their production was studying divinity, and by the repetition of the same expressions and imagery as were to be found in his own early poems. In these he pointed to fifteen alleged similarities. No one who will take the trouble to examine them with an impartial eye could now draw any such inference. The words and expressions which are said to support it are of so commonplace a character that, if this kind of reasoning had any claim to validity, no author would be safe. Even if a fair case for the repetition of similar expressions were made out, it would be more reasonable to attribute it to the peculiarities of style and the limits of diction which characterise every writer, and come into play equally in original work and in a free translation.

Scott wrote a sympathetic notice of Laing's work in the *Edinburgh Review*.[1] The great Lowlander had admired the poems early in life,

[1] July, 1805.

when, together with Spenser, they were put into
his hands by Blacklock ; but he found that they
ceased to charm when the first blush of youth
was over.   His opinion at the age of thirty-four
was most unfavourable to their authenticity ;
but he confessed that he was more at home in
the manners of the Border, than in the lore of
the Highlands and Celtic tradition.   From his
published opinion of Laing's work, and from a
private letter[1] written about the same time, it
is obvious that he based his judgment in a large
measure on Laing's arguments ; for he repeats
their substance and sometimes reproduces their
language.   He was, he said, "compelled to
admit that the greater part of the English
Ossian must be ascribed to Macpherson himself" ; and that after so much destructive criticism no one could now believe in Ossian as an
historical authority.   Scott, however, went so far
as to admit that before Macpherson there was
a general basis of tradition on which the poems,
whether collected or composed by himself, were
founded.   But he shared Laing's opinion that
the plagiarisms, especially from Milton, were
sufficiently obvious, that the description of

[1] Letter to Miss Seward, Lockhart's *Life*, ii. 53.

scenery and the romantic sentiment were Macpherson's own, and that in his prefaces he had intimated his own claim to the renown attending the alleged originals. Afterwards, however, on a tour in Skye, he records that friends of his there had heard parts of the poems in Gaelic recitations; but that both in Skye and elsewhere all agreed as to Macpherson's infidelity as a translator and editor.[1]

In August, 1804, the *Literary Journal*, an obscure periodical, had replied to Laing in a very spirited fashion, and some of the absurdities of his method were duly exposed in the preface to a translation of Gaelic poems which appeared at Liverpool in 1805. But his attack was more ably and more conclusively answered by Patrick Graham in an *Essay on the Authenticity of Ossian*, published in Edinburgh in 1807. Graham explained, as, indeed, Macpherson himself had indicated, that *Fingal* and *Temora* largely consisted of fragments and episodes for which there were authentic originals, skilfully interwoven, and bearing a distinct and definite character. He argued that any parallelisms of language between these and other poems, in

[1] Lockhart's *Life*, ii. 56, iii. 230.

itself antecedently probable, could at most prove
plagiarism as against the translation.   He refuted
the argument from the presence of occasional
rhymes by quoting a passage from Giraldus Cambrensis ; and he urged that if Macpherson had
imagined some historical connections which did
not exist—such as that between Caracul, the
Gaelic equivalent for " fierce-eyed," and Caracalla
—they could not affect the authenticity of the
poems as a whole ; and if the translator identified
the Balclutha of Ossian with the Alcuith of Bede,
it did not follow that there was no Balclutha.
He maintained, further, that their romantic sentiment was a fact highly favourable to their
genuineness.   Tacitus, who, through his father-
in-law Agricola, had excellent sources of knowledge, was on this point in thorough agreement
with Ossian ; and he had described the Caledonians of the third century as a refined, chivalrous
race, paying high respect to women, attaching
great value to their opinion, and alive to the
highest sentiments of valour and patriotism ; as
is more especially evident in the speech, for
which he must have had some foundation, put
into the mouth of Galgacus.[1]   The transmission

[1] See Tacitus, *Agricola*, xxv. *et seq. ; Ann.*, xiv., xxxiv.-v.

of the poems through many centuries was, in
Graham's opinion, easily explained by the fact
that the nation had, except to a slight extent,
remained unconquered by, and therefore unmingled with, any other people ; and that
consequently their language, as preserved by
their bards, had not appreciably altered.

The Report prepared by the Committee of the
Highland Society with great care and scrupulous
fairness was published in 1805, with an Appendix of letters, affidavits and Gaelic poems,
received in answer to certain queries which the
Committee had framed and addressed to various
persons throughout the Highlands.   The Report
and Appendix, besides disposing incidentally of
much previous criticism, form by far the most
important statement of the external evidence
bearing on the authenticity of the poems.   The
general character of the evidence will be apparent from the use made of it in the course of
this narrative.   The conclusion reached by the
Committee was :—

(i.) That a great legend of Fingal, and Ossian,
his son and songster, had immemorially existed
in Scotland ; and that Ossianic poetry, of an impressive and striking character, was to be found

generally and in great abundance in the Highlands; and that there were still, or until lately, many persons who could repeat large fragments of it.

(ii.) That while fragments had been found giving the substance and sometimes the literal expression of parts of Macpherson's work, no one poem was discoverable the same in title or tenor with his publications.

(iii.) That while the Committee inclined to believe that he supplied chasms and gave connections by inserting passages of his own, and that he added to the dignity and delicacy of the work by omitting or shortening certain incidents and refining the language, its members recognised that it was now impossible to determine how far these liberties extended; for Macpherson had enjoyed advantages which they did not possess, in that they made their investigation forty years later, when a search for Ossianic poetry was likely to be impeded or defeated by the change which had come over the Highlands during that period.

A large number of ancient MSS. and poems taken down from oral recitation had been sent to the Committee; and among them *The Dean of Lismore's Book.* From this ancient collection, of which some account has already been given,[1] the Committee inserted three poems in their Report, two attributed to Ossian, and one to Fergus his brother, and drew attention to the fact that of these poems two presented stories which Macpherson had embodied in his work, and the third agreed in tone and sentiment with the situation in which Ossian was there depicted. The Committee also took notice of other collectors contemporary with Macpherson; of Jerome Stone; of Dr. Smith of Campbelltown, who in 1780 published a prose version of Gaelic ballads, and in 1787 their originals; of Kennedy, who transcribed poems from oral recitation between 1778 and 1780; of Gillie, who issued others at Perth in 1786; and finally of Miss Brooke, who in 1789 brought out a metrical translation of Gaelic poems gathered in Ireland. The Committee remarked upon the important fact that these collections, the authenticity of which was undisputed, contained many passages nearly, and sometimes exactly, resembling parts of Macpherson's work; and that, although not always corresponding in title, story, and tenor

[1] See *supra,* pp. 104, 144-5.

of the narrative, their translations were generally marked by a similar strain of sublimity and tenderness.

Macpherson's originals and the thousand pounds sent from Indian admirers passed, on his death, to Mackenzie, who continued the preparations which Macpherson had made for the publication of the text. According to the account given by Sir John Sinclair, Dr. Ross of Edinburgh was employed to transcribe the whole of it over again, in order to settle the question of Gaelic orthography by following that adopted in the Gaelic Bible, with which all of those who read Gaelic were best acquainted. But no sooner were all arrangements made, and the first proofs delivered, than Mackenzie died. His executors resolved to hand the MS. over to the Highland Society of London ; and in 1807 it was duly published, with an entirely superfluous translation into Latin ; an interesting, and in some respects valuable, dissertation on the authenticity of the poems by Sir John Sinclair ; a translation of Cesarotti's essay on the same theme ; and supplementary essays, notes, and observations, by various hands.

To restore the text, and to present the old

poems in a form and language in which they would be intelligible to modern readers, had been Macpherson's acknowledged aim ; and with a similar object the text was re-edited after his death. Consequently, the language of the originals as they now stand is that which any educated Gael in the eighteenth century might have spoken, and no conclusion can be drawn from it as to the age of the fragments which they embodied. There is little room to doubt that a Gaelic text was invented for the interpolations and connections which the translator had himself supplied. But the precise and the concrete character of parts of the originals, where the English version is vague and general, or awkward and forced, and the fact that they contain some abstruse or corrupt passages which could not have been invented by any modern writer, make it obvious that a great, or perhaps the greater portion of them was built up out of genuine materials. In their style and structure Macpherson made a free use of what scholars call emendations, and what the incredulous call by a harsher name.[1]

[1] Dr. Ross' transcript is all that survives, as Macpherson's

The dissertation contained some fresh and
interesting evidence, and an account, which
appears to be perfectly trustworthy, of a large
collection of Gaelic poems made by one John
Farquharson, some years previous to the rising
of '45.   According to the testimony of Dr.
Cameron, Bishop of Edinburgh, and four Roman
Catholic priests, this Farquharson, afterwards
Prefect of Studies at Douay, filled a thick
folio volume with Gaelic poems current in the
neighbourhood of Strathglass, Inverness-shire,
when he was serving his time as a missionary.
This volume he took with him to Douay, and
there it was often seen by the five persons above
mentioned between 1763 and 1777.   When
Macpherson's translations were sent to him at

MS., at one time in the Advocates' Library, unaccountably
disappeared.   Sir David Brewster had access to his papers ;
and he declared (see note to Art. "Ossian," *Edinb. Encycl.*,
1830) that there was not the slightest trace of evidence
among them that Macpherson had either composed the
poems or wished others to believe that he had composed
them.   There was nothing which could throw any light
on the points in dispute, except a diary.   I have been informed by his grandson's widow that this diary, which is
said to have contained some information as to the collection
of the poems, and was, by reason of other contents, carefully guarded by the family, was stolen, probably by a
servant, shortly after Sir David Brewster's death in 1868.

Douay in 1766, Farquharson declared that he had all that Macpherson had and much more. The manuscript was seen in a torn condition in 1777, but it was destroyed with the rest of the Douay Library in the burning of the College during the French Revolution.

The effect of this publication and of the work done by the Highland Society was to bring much of the controversy to an end ; although the discussion continued for many years in various parts of Scotland and on the Continent. Attempts have since been made to revive a general interest in it, but without success ; partly because in more recent times the poems have ceased to be read. Subsequent opinion has, on the whole, tended to confirm the conclusion at which the Committee arrived ; and while critical inquiry has established proofs, unnecessarily numerous and severe, that Macpherson's Celtic history is over-sanguine fiction, that he was grossly inaccurate as an editor and translator, and that in both these capacities he made a very full use of the licence permitted to a poet, some evidence has also been obtained in further support of the general authenticity of the bulk of his work. More Gaelic poems were collected, and fresh

efforts made to bear out Macpherson's contention.

To describe them all would be a tedious
task, but the following contributions to the
controversy deserve to be mentioned. In
1825 an interesting *Essay* on the authenticity
of the poems was published at Ayr by Lieut.
Donald Campbell; and in 1841 the *Genuine
Remains of Ossian* were brought out in a
new translation by Macgregor, who in his introduction summarised the evidence then ac-
cessible. In 1862 there appeared a selection
from *The Dean of Lismore's Book*, with translation and notes by MacLauchlan, and an introduction by the late Mr. Skene. About the same
time Campbell of Islay published his *Popular
Tales of the West Highlands*, in which he discussed the Ossianic question at great length.
He afterwards came to a conclusion very unfavourable to Macpherson, as may be gathered
from his *Leabhar na Feinne*, published some ten
years later. In 1868 Dr. Ebrard, a learned
German, who enjoyed the advantage of undisputed impartiality, defended Macpherson with
great skill and ingenuity in an essay appended
to his *Ossians Finnghal*, a metrical translation of

the poems. In 1870 a last attempt was made to establish the antique character of every line of Macpherson's originals, and to defend their claim to be descended from the third century, in a fine edition of the *Poems of Ossian*, edited and translated by Archibald Clerk, whose prefatory essay is the best general defence of so extreme and untenable an opinion. It was attacked by various eminent scholars, and among them by Campbell, who in a page of the *Times*[1] brought the learning and research of forty years to bear against its conclusions. In 1875 Dr. Hately Waddell, in his *Ossian and the Clyde*, a work full of minute, original and ingenious knowledge, adduced a great array of geological, geographical and etymological facts, to prove that the poems of Ossian were authentic and historical. In the nature of the poems themselves, and in the circumstances under which they were produced, there was plenty of material for rival theories ; and the combatants on one side and on the other did no more than form their judgments on partial views of multifarious and intricate evidence.

When all has been said, one thing is clear.

[1] 15th April, 1871.

In spite of the tawdry effect of its modern
setting, Macpherson's collection displays a rich
vein of that wayward, sensitive, and melancholy
genius of the Celt which is for us an ancient
source of inspiration.   Much that is best in our
romantic literature has been drawn from it.   At
an early stage of the controversy it was said that
there was more real poetic feeling in these old
Gaelic pieces than could have come from a rude
nation, and from an age so turbulent and so remote.   This is a line of reasoning which we have
long forsaken.   The origins of poetry elude our
search and baffle our arguments ; but we know
that among races which we are accustomed to
regard as uncivilised, poems of great length and
complexity have been transmitted from mouth
to mouth for centuries.   Analogies, though they
prove nothing, are useful if they enlarge our
understanding.   The epic songs of the Finns
have also come to us by oral tradition alone ;
they have preserved from an almost fabulous
antiquity a strain of high poetic genius ; and
if we are to refer them to a single person,
Wainamoïnen excites our amazement no less
than Ossian.   When Lönnrot fused these
songs into a definite whole and produced the

Kalevala, an epic poem as long as the *Iliad*, and as rounded and complete, it was nowhere challenged, although its materials had been handed down from a mythical age. The ancient Highlanders, as they are described by Tacitus, and as we can trace them for ourselves in the remains of their activity,—in the vitrified forts, the sculptured stones, and the rude beginnings of decorative art [1] that still survive, are as likely as the Finns to have originated poetry of an heroic cast. Its mournful tone may be the echo of a struggle against an overwhelming aggressor, tempered and refined by the influence of Druids and bards.

There is no lack of more ambitious analogies, such as might perhaps be drawn from the Homeric poems, if scholars could agree upon their history; or from the Indian epics, if all that we know of their nature and the legend of their formation is true. But if we keep to the popular epics of the North and the West of Europe, a more fruitful comparison may be established with the *Edda* or the *Nibelungenlied;* so far, that is, as their history is concerned, for no other comparison could here be

[1] See Archibald Clerk, *op. cit.,* i. xxxv.

21

attempted. In the older *Edda* we have a collection of poems orally recited by the Icelandic Skalds, which were committed to writing and fused, or, it may be, partly composed by Sigfusson in the eleventh century. From these and other materials Snorro-Sturleson, a hundred and fifty years later, produced an *Edda* in prose, which has not yet been denounced as spurious. The work that was done on the Scandinavian ballads by these two Icelanders is substantially the work that was done by Macpherson on the Gaelic poetry of the Highlands. And it is further to be observed, that just as the matter which he collected and his own additions were turned again into verse by various hands, so Oehlenschläger drew on the prose *Edda* for his *Gods of the North.*

In respect of some of their external features, and of the controversy which they have aroused, the parallel between the Ossianic poems, as Macpherson left them, and the *Nibelungenlied* in the form in which it has come to us from the close of the twelfth century, is curiously exact. The matter of both is a mixture of myth and of history, and both are based on songs and ballads of uncertain date and origin. In the one and in the other a fresh and alien element is super-induced; in the *Nibelungenlied* the ideas of the age of chivalry refine the gods and heroes of an early mythology: in the Ossianic poems, a literary elegance obscures what was rough and harsh in the old Celtic legends. In either it cannot be determined how much was drawn from ancient lore and how much was added by the collector; but there seems to be as good a case for the authenticity of the Ossianic poems, as for that of the *Edda* or the *Nibelungenlied;* and with the old writers who gave those works to the world, Macpherson is fairly entitled to rank.

THE END.

INDEX OF NAMES.

Lessing, 20 note.
Lönnrot, 320.
Louth's *Nature of Hebrew Poetry*, 82.
Lyttelton, Lord, 89, 179.

Macaulay, 193, 229 note.
MacCodrum, 125.
Macdonald, Alex., 57.
MacIntyre, Dr., of Glenorchay, 141.
Mackenzie, Henry, 181 note, 303.
Mackenzie, John, 279, 290-2, 314.
    ,,   ,, letter to, 279.
Mackintosh of Borlum, 281.
Maclagan, James, letters to, 146, 152, 154.
Macleod, Prof., 135.
Macleod, Dr. Donald, 121.
Macmhuirichs, the, 126 *et seq.*
Macnicol's *Remarks on Dr. Johnson's Tour*, 255-6.
Macpherson, Alex., *Glimpses of Church and Social Life in the Highlands*, 32 note, 237 note.
Macpherson, Ewen, 124, 129.
Macpherson, James, his parentage, 32; birth, 33; education, 36; goes to Aberdeen, 39, and to Edinburgh, 42; returns to Ruthven as schoolmaster, 43; his early poetry, 45, 61; *The Hunter* and *The Highlander*, 46-7; contributes to the *Scots Magazine*, 48; collects Gaelic poetry, 59; becomes a tutor, 63; meets John Home at Moffat, 66; translates a Gaelic fragment, 68; goes to Edinburgh and meets Blair, 74; who urges him to further translation,

77; publishes the *Fragments*, 78; undertakes a mission to the Highlands, 94; his first journey, 117; his second, 147; returns to Edinburgh, 149; is assisted by Blair, 149; proposes to publish the originals, 154; goes to London, 158; publishes *Fingal*, 161; and *Temora*, 189; behaves foolishly, 200; goes to Florida, 213; returns to write for the press, 213; writes his *Introduction to the History of Great Britain and Ireland*, 217; translates the *Iliad*, 220; which fails, 223; continues ⸗ Hume's *History*, 225; visits Paris, 227; publishes a fourth edition of the poems, 239; is attacked by Johnson, 244; writes to Strahan, 245; replies to Johnson, and threatens him, 248; publishes the *Original Papers*, 228; and his *History of Great Britain*, 231; supervises the Court newspapers, 233; writes against the American claims, 259; and with Sir John Macpherson attacks the East India Company, 262; becomes agent to the nabob of Arcot, 270; enters the House of Commons, 273; receives money from Indian admirers wherewith to print his originals of Ossian, 279; fate of the money, 314; builds a house in Badenoch, 281; joins the Whigs, 284; prepares to publish the originals, 289; his chil-